Developing Proficient Readers
Teach Model and Model

Developing Proficient Readers Teach Model and Model

Mrs. Shonisani Agnes Mulovhedzi

Prof. N. P. Mudzielwana

GYAN

First Published, 2018

Published by

Gyan Publishing House
5, Ansari Road
Daryaganj, New Delhi-110002
Phone: 9811692060
E-mail: books@gyanbooks.com

Printed at: G. Print Process, Delhi.

Cataloging in Publication Data—DK
Courtesy: D.K. Agencies (P) Ltd. <docinfo@dkagencies.com>

Mulovhedzi, Shonisani Agnes, author.
Developing proficient readers teach model and model / Mrs. Shonisani Agnes Mulovhedzi, Prof. N.P. Mudzielwana.
pages cm
Includes bibliographical references.
ISBN 9788121213608

1. Leadership—Study and teaching (Early childhood) 2. Reading (Early childhood) I. Mudzielwana, N. P., author. II. Title.

LCC HM1261.M85 2017 | DDC 372.8 23

I dedicate this book to my husband Tshitereke Ronald Mudzielwana and my children Mukhethwa, Mudzunga and Khathutshelo and my grandchildren

Contents

Acknowledgement

The authors would like to thank the following people who proved to be indispensable in the selfless way they supported us:

- Our dear Spouses, Mr Nthambeleni Eric Mulovhedzi and Mr Tshitereke Ronald Mudzielwanafor their support and advice during the writing process.
- We extend our heartfelt appreciation to the principals and teachers who shared their expertise with us and valuable input.
- The education officials who gave us permission to access the schools
- Marketing and editorial departments of Gyan Publishing House for bringing out readable book through their expertise and experience.

Foreword

The Department of Basic Education is committed to ensuring to produce learners that are able to identify and solve problems and make decisions using critical and creative thinking; work effectively as individuals and with others as members of a team; organise and manage themselves and their activities responsibly and effectively; collect, analyse, organise and critically evaluate information; communicate effectively using visual, symbolic and/or language skills in various modes; use science and technology effectively and critically showing responsibility towards the environment and the health of others; and demonstrate an understanding of the world as a set of related systems by recognising that problem solving contexts do not exist in isolation. This book is timely in that it is a means that subserves the interest of the Foundation Phase teachers to teach different leadership skills at a tender age.

Our aim through this book is to provide high quality and harmonized early leadership skills education for all children. The early years are critical in children's leadership development. It is the period when they develop rapidly, assimilating leadership key skills that enabling them to flourish throughout their school years and beyond. This book includes different ideas from teacher about the developing proficient readers teach model and model. Its principal aim is to help Foundation Phase teachers to impart leadership skills to all children during early years of learning.

Preface

The idea of this book developed from our frustration with the lack of student leaders in the higher education.This book sets out the importance of teaching leadership skills at a very important stage of child development. In our quest to promote the harmonious leadership skills development of young learners, this book provide teachers with a set of understanding leadership as terminology.

The purpose of developing leadership skills to young learners could mold them to be a responsible adult. The content of this book discusses some of the critical issues in leadership, such as focusing on the common leadership education challenges that teachers face in teaching leadership skills with the necessary ethics, value and character among learners from an early age.In compiling this book, care has been taken to present the information in an applied and practical form, reflecting both the field itself and its unique South African context.

We have enjoyed writing this book. It has been challenging and thought provoking and has enhanced our own understanding. We hope it will become a corner stone of teachers in teaching leadership skills to young learners to develop future leaders. It will enhance teachers' understanding of young learner's learning through coping their leadership behaviour.

Mrs Shonisani Agnes Mulovhedzi and
Professor Ndileleni Paulinah Mudzielwana
School of Education
Department of Early Childhood Education
University of Venda

Introduction

Leadership skills from the earlies days of civilisation to modern times have been essential to all aspects of life including educational institutions. Teachers expected to develop learners with the knowledge of different leadership skills to orient them to early learning and beyond and to build future leaders in the global society. Currently, growing job market demands leaders to fill positions in different organisations. Teachers in the classroom, focus on teaching learners without considering the development of leadership skills in early grades. Policycommitted to ensuring to produce learners that are able to show different leadership behaviour from an early age.

Foundation phase is the stage that includes Grade R – Grade 3. At this age learners are curious and want to explore their school environments and play either on their own or with others. It is here that the role of the leadership behaviour of the learners is of prime significance. This book aim at providing teachers with a broad framework which gives ample space and flexibility to devise and carry out leadership activities based on the experiences and needs of the learners. Leadership activities must take place in an atmosphere of joy, trust and love in order to develop long lasting skills on learners.

This book is thus intended to help foundation phase teachers plan to meet the variousleadership needs of the learners, so that most will achieve and others, where appropriate, will go beyond the early learning leadership goal before entry into intermediate phase.

To help teachers, this book provides for most appropriate ideas for importance of teaching leadership skills to encourage the behaviour of the effective leaders and discouraged the behaviour of the bullies during teaching and learning activities.Teachers should show the ability to form strong relationships in order to instill leadership skills in learners. Learners should be regularly encouraged to build their leadership skills so that they can assert themselves in school and also outside in the world. Leadership is vital in the classroom as it assists learners to become involved and work as teamleaders.

Chapter - 1

Developmental and Learning Theories

Introduction

All learning theories are rooted in the philosophical, social and political context of time and influence the way we teach children (Tracy and Morrow, 2006:15). Ever since education began and became formalised it appears that teachers have been engaged in determining how children develop and learn. For this reason, several educationalists and psychologists have developed systemic, yet contrasting, theories of learning. Each learning theory implies a set of related classroom procedures. Theories help us to understand the foundations of teaching and learning. They shed light on the nature of the learning problems encountered by the learners. They offer a basis for instructional methods. Those who teach without theories may follow the road that leads nowhere. Scientist has many definitions of the concept theory. Theory has been defined as a provisional systemisation of events enabling us to see the relationships among facts. Another definition views a theory as a human convention for keeping data in order. A theory could also be viewed as a possible world that can be checked against the real world. All views of theory reflect our needs to organise information and make sense out of life (Osipow *et al.,* 1980:24).

Teacher's teaching practice maybe influenced by these psychological views on the teaching of reading comprehension. Consequently, teachers who support a specific learning theory make professional decisions based on this theory, which in turn, affects their classroom procedures.

In their view, Bigge and Shermis (1999) define learning theories and their importance in teaching and learning as:

> *designed for the development of a pattern of ideas accompanied by a planned procedure carrying it out. Hence, it is a policy proposed and followed as a basis for action. A learning theory, then, is a systematic integrated outlook in regard to the nature of the process whereby people relate to their environment in such a way as to enhance their ability to use both themselves and their environments in a most effective way* (Bigge and Shermis, 1999: 2-3).

The constructivist learning theories are important because they indicate that teachers cannot provide learners with knowledge. In a learning situation, learners must be able to construct knowledge in their own minds (Slavin, 1994). In this research project, the act of comprehending texts was seen as both a cognitively and socially constructed process. This is the reason why the four mentioned theories Piaget (1983), Vygotsky (1978), Bruner (1986), Ausubel (1963) and Bandura (1977) serve as a basis of the study. Constructivists encourage children to constantly use prior knowledge to understand new information.

The various theories discussed in this chapter serve as a point of reference for appreciating the various stages and processes of the child and how these stages affect their development and learning capacities (Mooney, 2000). These theories may assist teachers to explore the research-based strategies that brought about success stories in other countries. These strategies could be helpful to the teachers because learners do not learn at the same pace. The theories may assist teachers to consciously plan and teach learners how to use strategies independently. These theories have influenced current notions of the teaching of reading comprehension and have also informed this study. These guidelines will help the teachers on how to teach learners not just to bark at print, but to read the text with understanding and therefore become proficient readers.

In this chapter various theories of Piaget (1983), Vygotsky (1978), Bruner (1986), Ausubel (1963), Bandura (1977) and Gardner will be discussed. Even though they vary greatly, each articulates a similar context of learning and development. Eggen and Kauchak (2001) state that while constructivists see learning as an active process that requires learners to construct meaning, social constructivism suggests that knowledge exists in a social context and is initially shared with others instead of being represented solely in the mind of the individual.

Developmental Learning Theories

Knowledge of child development is important when planning to teach. It is essential for the teacher to understand the particular life stage of the individuals for which learning interventions are planned. Haas and Parkey (1993:108) endorse this when they state that being conversant with developmental theories provides '... a point of view with reference to learners: they should be studied as individuals so that the programme of institutions can be shaped in part, by the individuals' own nature and needs'. It is important for the teacher to understand the learners' individual, physical, emotional, social and cognitive abilities and limitations so that appropriate teaching strategies related to reading comprehension can be implemented.

Though all aspects of human development are important and interdependent, the cognitive development of the learner in the Foundation Phase should be taken into consideration. It pertains to the learners' mental capacities and specifically the intellectual abilities that are involved in thinking, knowledge and problem solving, in relation to the age of the individual and the information to be imparted (Mwamwenda, 1995:89). Cognitive development occurs progressively as it builds on previous experience and teachers should provide reading comprehension strategies, such as problem-based learning experiences.

The family is the most important early influence on the socialisation of the learner. Social development starts in the home and expands as the child's interpersonal contacts extend outside the family. Children begin to learn how to adapt to other people at home, and then apply their skills to the schools and broader community environment as they venture into the outside world. The early influence of values, attitudes, worldview and modes of adaptation at home directly affects how children cope with the environment of the school

(Mwamwenda, 1995:55-56). Social experience is important, because at school the learner is expected to relate to the teachers, follow a new set of rules, make new friends and learn to get along with them successfully.

Learners need to acquire the cognitive and behavioural skills necessary for school success. These skills and others are learnt in and out of the classroom, at home and in the community (Cortese and Middleton, 1994:166; Louw, 1993, 1991:13). Cooperative learning is one strategy to use to encourage learners to work together on a particular reading comprehension project (Bender, 1997:72-73). Emotionally, the Foundation Phase learners are greatly influenced by the interpersonal climate in the school. They may experience fear if the school atmosphere is unfriendly and hostile and if they are humiliated, shouted at or physically punished. Walsh and Murphy (2003:14-15) state that a negative atmosphere which also includes exclusive competitiveness and is associated with poor academic performance of the learners.

There are many theories. Each theory has an influence on the teaching of reading.

Piaget's Theory of Cognitive Development

Cognitive theories of learning have their origin in Piaget's view on children's development. Piaget (1959:79) states that: "each child has his own world of hypotheses and solutions which has never communicated to anyone, language is moulded on habits and thoughts". Jean Piaget (1968) has provided one of the most comprehensive descriptions of children's cognitive capabilities and development. Piaget's theory is based on a number of assumptions, which underpin the way in which he believed children learn (Kail, 2001:150-152). He maintained that children use schemes to organise, categorise and understand the world. As children grow older, these schemes become increasingly abstract as new experiences are assimilated into the existing schemes. Piaget used the term 'accommodation' to refer to the process of reorganising existing schemes to improve the new information so that equilibrium is achieved. If accommodation does not occur, then disequilibrium occurs and children have to organise their schemes to achieve equilibrium. Piaget states that experiences and interaction with the environment, and not only maturation, that facilitate the development of cognitive structures (Lieberman, Clark, Krone, Orlandi and Wynder, 1992:392). According to Piaget, children's cognitive development progresses sequentially through a series of stages which are linked to certain age ranges. The transition from the sensory motor stage through the preoperational, concrete operational and formal operational stages can be seen as a continuum on which children move from subjective to objective realisation (Gage and Berliner, 1992:105-116).

For Piaget, learning is a process of internal construction. Learners must construct knowledge in their own minds through the guidance of more knowledgeable others. Teachers must teach learners to acquire self-regulatory competence by observing and hearing their explanations. For example, when the teacher is demonstrating the use of the strategy, guiding and giving constructive feedback the learners use the self-directing, self-pacing and self-correcting strategy and learn how to adjust their skill to change personal, behavioural and contextual conditions to optimise their own learning during reading.

Piaget concluded that cognitive growth occurs in a series of invariant and interdependent stages. At each stage, the child is capable of learning only certain cognitive tasks. In essence, the child's ability to think and learn changes with age. In a way, that is, with passage through a series of maturational or developmental stages. The quantity, quality, depth, and breadth of learning that occurs are functions of the stages during which the learning takes place.

Piaget provides the following schematic description of the normal child's stages of development:

1. The first two years of life through their sense and movements and by interacting with the physical environment. By moving, touching, hitting, biting, and so on and by physically manipulating objects, children learn about the properties of space, time, location, permanence and causality.
2. Piaget called the next five years of life, ages two to seven years the preoperational stage. During this stage children

make intuitive judgements about relationships and also begin to think with symbols. Language becomes increasingly important and children learn to use symbols to represent the concrete world. Their thinking is dominated by the world of perception.

3. The period between ages seven and eleven is called the concrete operational stage. During this stage, children are able to think through relationships, to perceive consequences of acts and to group entities in a logical fashion. Their thinking are shaped by previous experiences and depend on concrete objects that they have manipulated through the senses.
4. The fourth stage is called formal operational stage and commences from eleven. This stage reflects a major transition in the thinking process. During this stage, children develop the capacity to work with abstractions, theories and logical relationship without having to refer to the concrete.

The Concrete Operational

This stage lasting from seven to eleven years of age as promoted by Piaget. During this stage, children start to use logical thought processes, such as reversal of concepts, multiple classifications and mental ordering, to begin to solve problems limited to real, observable objects. Centralisation is no longer present during this stage as children begin to realise that there are many sides to a particular problem (Mwamwenda, 1995:95-100; Biehler and Snowman, 1993:61-66; Vasta, Haith and Miller, 1995:35).

Some key principles of contemporary cognitive learning theories guide instruction. Such instruction must be constructive, link new information to prior knowledge, be given in a guiding social environment, teach strategies, develop automation, and involve motivated student.

Learning is a constructive process. Knowledge cannot be given directly to students instead, each person must construct or build his or her own knowledge. The abilities to acquire knowledge depends in part of whether the student already knows enough to have an internal cognitive structure that he or she can use to take in and interpret new information. For example, a child who knows that 2 + 2 = 4 can learn the new number fact, 2 + 3 more easily if it is linked to the existing schema of 2 + 2.

Learning is Linking New Information to Prior Knowledge

Learning is a cumulative process that depends on prior knowledge and past experiences. The more one knows about a subject, the more one can acquire through a learning experience. What students learn depends on the experiences they bring to the learning situation. Since new knowledge is built on what is already known, students must learn to use as the experience, knowledge, and skills they already possess.

Teacher should start with what students already know, and then help them to build and link new information. In reading, this might mean using the student's existing knowledge of words, books, and stories as the starting point of teaching reading.

Learning Requires Instruction at the Appropriate Level and a Guiding Social Environment

A critical element of learning is the social and reciprocal relationship between the teacher and the student. The teacher serves as a guide for the student, providing the information and support necessary for the student to learn and grow intellectually. This support is referred to as scaffolding because student use this help while they build a firm understanding that will eventually allow them to solve the problem or accomplish the task on their own.

Learning is Strategic

Many students with learning disabilities believe that learning require sheer memory, such as remembering words, numbers, or facts. The problem is not usually one of limited memory capacities. Because ineffective learners lack knowledge of strategies to perform learning tasks, they employ a generally disorganised approach to cognitive assignments. Significant differences are found between good and poor learners in their knowledge about learning strategies. The research shows that poor students often do very well when taught to use a strategy.

Learning Requires Automaticity in Some Skills

For students with learning disabilities, the flow of information is hampered because they have difficulty acquiring the automatisation needed for successful learning. Through automatisation, certain knowledge becomes almost subconscious, requiring little processing efforts. Successful reading, for example, requires rapid and fluent recognition of words. For efficient learning to take place, many areas performance must become automatic and habitual responses to stimuli. Example of such are automatic include remembering words when speaking, inserting the proper syntactic word form in sentences, and remembering words by sight when reading. Some student with reading disabilities cannot quickly recall words, colours, numbers and pictures.

Learning Requires Motivation

Motivation energises and directs behaviour. It is the drive to accomplish goals and, in education, the desire to learn. Much of school learning requires hard work over a long period of time. It requires students to be active, involved, committed, and interested over a sustained period of time. They must be goal oriented and work hard to figure out the meaning of what they read or to solve an arithmetic problem. To maintain motivation, teachers must make learning enjoyable and show pleasure in their student's successes.

Piaget's theory has implications for teaching reading comprehension, as each individual child's current stage of cognition development must be taken into account when the teacher plans learning activities. The theory helps teachers to understand that learners at this level have reached a new level of self-development that allows them to understand some of the ways in which they are related to people. Through interaction with the teacher and other persons, and during play, learners are able to understand the physical and the social world. Here, realistic fiction may encourage learners to interact with characters who are involved in a conflict situation, during reading comprehension. Knowledge about this stage will assist the teacher to understand that the learners are ready to listen to stories and to read about real-life heroes and stories which move between the past and present, such as legends.

The knowledgeable teacher is aware that learners in this stage begin to apply logic to concrete experience, so that they begin to move beyond one-dimensional thinking. In regard to reading comprehension, this enables learners to relate one event to a system of interrelated parts. They gradually start perceiving an event from the beginning to the end and from the conclusion to the beginning. It is therefore important that the environment should be rich to encourage learners to learn and reason about what they read. Learners at this stage have the ability to understand picture storybooks, folk tales, and books written for bibliotherapy. It is critical for the teacher to guide learners on which strategies to use, showing them when and why and how to apply each strategy correctly.

Piaget's theory relates to this study because reading text should match the developmental stages of learners. Learners should construct the meaning of the text and be able to use it in contexts other than the classroom. Learning activities should match the level of the conceptual development of the learners. The teacher must use the stages as a way to gauge and monitor learners' pace of learning. Piaget's view is that learners must be self-initiated and actively involved in learning. In reading comprehension, teachers must be able to model good behaviour of reading with understanding so that learners will ultimately take responsibility for their own learning. Although Piaget focused on cognition, he also emphasised the importance of the environment in learning, particularly the social environment. In reading development may be influenced by interactions with others. The learners see and hear the teachers and peers reading and then internalise and model what they see and hear.

Vygotsky's Socio-historical Theory of Cognitive Development

Lev Vygotsky (1978) attributed cognitive development to the social environment of the child. The social context and cognition can influence each other in the learning process. . in this process the learners is able to construct knowledge in his/her mind through cognitive and social process (Conley, duPlessis, 2007:3).Vygotsky noted that children begin learning from the behaviours, attitudes, values and skills of the people around them. Vygotsky believed that cognitive development begins with social interaction and then directs itself inward. The social world and one's culture determine which stimuli occur and are attended to. Vygotsky emphasised the role of adults in influencing the cognitive development of children. Development is enhanced when children work cooperatively or collaboratively with adults and other children. Cognitive development proceeds from behaviours regulated by others to self-regulated behaviour (Zimmerman, 1998). To help children move from a social to a personal psychological form of knowledge, adults should determine the child's actual development level by learning about his capacity to solve problems when working with or without adult help.

According to Vygotsky, when a child is working independently, we see the actual development level of the child. When the child is working with an adult, we see the potential development of the child, under optimal circumstances, while learning with a competent nurturing mediator. The difference between these two levels of functioning is referred to as the Zone of Proximal Development (ZPD) (Biehler and Snowman, 1993:63; Gage and Berliner, 1992:122-123). In regard to the importance of the ZPD, Vygotsky (1998:137-138) emphasised:

> *everything that the child cannot do independently, but which he can be taught or which he can do with direction or cooperation or with the help of leading questions, we will include in the sphere of imitation... Thus, in studying what the child is capable of doing independently, we study yesterday's development. Studying what the child is capable of doing cooperatively, we ascertain tomorrow's development.*

The area of immature, but maturing processes makes up the child's ZPD. When children are faced with challenging situations, they can seek help from their teachers and peers, which is termed 'scaffolding' (Woolfolk, 1995:50).

Vygotsky believed that language is an important tool because it is internalised by the child to affect thinking and problem-solving (Bukatko and Daehner, 2001:27; Shaffer 1996:279). The role of the adult is to assist children to acquire language in ways that enable them to take control of their own learning (Engelbrecht and Green,

2001:84). Teachers can focus on effective communication, meaning, comprehension and respect for language in the classroom. Vygotsky's theory has implications for teaching reading comprehension because in facilitating learning, the teacher must take the cultural context of the learners into consideration as it influences their thinking and actions. Learners can be given problem-solving activities with instructions, for the task of reading comprehension. Thereafter the learner should work independently using his or her own knowledge and skills with the guidance received from the teacher. Two approaches are pertinent to teaching reading comprehension, based on the views of Vygotsky, namely reciprocal teaching and scaffolded support.

Scaffold Support

Scaffolding is a sub-skill of metacognition. A teacher provides scaffolding, offering support that is gradually withdrawn as learners become capable of doing for themselves. In the context of the present study this refers to providing and adjusting assistance according to a reader's performance. This adjustment may occur within a session (such as within a guided reading session) as well as across a session (such as from modelled to guided independent reading) (Graves and Graves, 1994). According to the research in this area, teacher assistance with a reader's learning can be successful only when a shared understanding or "intersubjectivity" is established between the teacher and the student (Fournier and Graves, 2003). To find a common ground for communication, a teacher needs to discover what the reader understands and then decide what assistance will work best in each case (Bodrova and Leong, 1996). It seems that intersubjectivity is a valuable precursor to internationalisation of language. Once intersubjectivity is established, a teacher can gradually reduce control of the reading act and children may become more able to function independently as readers (Barchers, 1998).

Bruner (1998) emphasises the importance of scaffolding that is, building an instructional structure that assists in the learning process. In other words, expert teachers should create environments that scaffold students' learning and maximise students' opportunities to learn.

Vyotsky's (1978) socio-cultural theory has brought researchers to the realisation that children live in rich social contexts that affect the way their cognitive world is structured (Rogoff, 1998). Vygotsky (1978) believed that complex mental activities such as reading have theory origins in social interactions. through various activities with knowledgeable adults, children come to master activities. Vygotsky's (1978) Zone of Proximal Development (ZPD) explains how the process happens. It refers to a range of activities that the learners cannot handle alone, but can be able to do only with the help of the more knowledgeable person. Scaffolding involves the provision of support that is focused on a learner's particular capacities within Vygotsky's ZPD. When teaching reading, teachers need to shift the responsibility to the learners at some time, gradually releasing responsibility to learners so that they learn to master their own learning. Teachers take all the responsibilities for applying a newly introduced strategy by modelling. Learners in turn must observe, imitate practices and then self-regulate themselves and create meaning from the written text by using the strategy appropriately. As time goes on and learners get more exposure and practice using the strategies, the teacher steps back, allowing the child to take over their responsibility for the task at hand. This is to enable learners to manage their own learning by making use of the strategies. Teachers work collaboratively with the learners and the strategy, giving and taking as much as necessary to create meaning. Eventually, learners take more and more responsibility as they become confident, knowledgeable and capable; finally, they are able to work independently (Pardo, 2004:278; McMahon and Oliver, 2003:5). Shanahan (2006) refers to the gradual release of responsibility as the 'I do it–We do it–You do it' approach to teaching reading comprehension. According to Shanahan (2006), this can benefit the learners if the teacher provides guidance beforehand. What is important is the support given to learners, the available resources and appropriate activities for engaging them.

Reciprocal Teaching (RT)

Teaching reading has been a challenge for decades. To address the challenge, Palincsar and Brown (1984) developed an approach to teaching reading comprehension called reciprocal teaching.

Reciprocal teaching is a co-operative learning activity intended to boost comprehension. Reciprocal teaching is an instructional procedure to improve learners' comprehension skills and is related to Vygotsky's ZPD and scaffolding (Lysynchuk and Vye, 1990). This approach has three main components, namely, dialogue between learners and teacher, each taking a turn in the role of dialogue leader. After a section of the text read, one learner:

> *Summarises what has just been read, ask two or three questions, clarifies details and predicts what will be said. Reciprocal interactions is where one person acts in response to other and structured dialogue using four strategies, namely generating one's own questions, summarising parts of the text, clarifying word meanings and confusing text passages, and predicting what might come next in the text.*

In a similar way the reciprocal teaching approach, Palincsar and Brown (1984), (1985) allows students to use language as a tool for learning and for scaffolding the learning of others. Social interaction allows students to experience 'cognitive apprenticeship' (Roth and Bowen, 1995), a related application of group works that recognises the value of social interaction in the use of experts to scaffold novices' learning.

Reciprocal teaching of reading was one of the first strategy based reading programmes to exemplify an information-processing view of comprehension (Palincsar and Brown, 1994). It is a group questioning technique where the teacher and students take turns leading group or class discussion, regarding the content of texts they are reading or listening to. Initially the teacher models and labels different comprehension strategies to help guide the leader's discussion: questioning, summarising, clarifying and predicting (Roth-Smith, 2000, p. 394). The ensuing discussion is directed towards text content, inferences, disagreements in interpretation, arriving at a general summary of the segment read and a prediction of what will come next.

In developing the RTR technique Palincsar and Brown (1984) identified six information processing prerequisites for good reading comprehension: (a) understanding the purpose for reading; (b) activating relevant background knowledge; (c) discerning essential from unessential information; (d) evaluating reading material for consistency; (e) monitoring comprehension; and (f) drawing and testing inferences from text. However, as Nicaise and Gettinger (1995) report Palincsar and Brown's (1985) focus was on the modelling and coaching in four reading strategies: question-formulation, text summarisation, text clarification and prediction.

RTR consists of a number of distinct steps. To begin with both the teacher and the students read an assigned paragraph silently. Following this, the teacher models the strategies of formulating questions, constructing a summary, clarifying difficult information and making a prediction. Each student then takes on the role of "teacher," while the actual teacher offers coaching on how to perform the strategy. The teacher's input fades as the students become increasingly competent.

This approach is heavily dependent on the students 'ability to model the teacher's cognitive activities. A Meta Language Awareness Programme involving reciprocal teaching (1985) focuses on student-to-student and teacher-to-student interaction, critical aspects of effective comprehension and content instruction. "It is through discussion that the teacher learns what is in the students' minds, and thereby can restructure the situation to aid the student in understanding" (Flood and Lapp, 1990:493).

Reciprocal teaching takes place through scaffolded instruction of four comprehension-fostering and comprehension-monitoring strategies. In reciprocal teaching, these strategies pertain to ongoing dialogues with a dialogue leader, who can be a teacher or a learner who models the use of the strategies, provides conditional knowledge about strategy use, and helps learners to apply a strategy to a passage. As the learners in the group become familiar with the strategies and the procedure, the dialogue leader's involvement lessens and learners take turns as discussions leaders. The assumption is that by applying the strategies in a group process, poorly self-regulated learners can learn from their highly self-regulated peers.

The overall goal of reciprocal teaching is to promote self-directed and flexible use of the learnt strategies through scaffolding instruction collaboration (Sporer *et al.,* 2009:273). According to the NRP (2000), reading comprehension is the construction of meaning of a written text through the reciprocal interchange of ideas between the reader and the message in particular. It has been described as a gradual release or transfer of control or responsibility (Palincsar and Brown, 1984; Shanahan, 2006). According to the NRP (2000), the focus of reciprocal teaching is upon the actual teaching approach, which is relevant to this study. Reciprocal teaching involves four instructional procedures for explicitly teaching four strategies namely, summarising, questioning, clarifying and predicting (Palincsar and Brown, 1984). The NRP (2000:22) explicitly describes the reciprocal teaching procedure. The teacher begins with a group of learners discussing the text. The teacher starts by modelling each strategy. The demonstration includes a clear explanation of what the strategy is, a description of how and when to use it, and an explanation of why it is useful for enhancing understanding. After explaining and modelling the strategy, the teacher asks learners to read, providing an abundance of guidance and support (Zimmerman, 1998; Shanahan, 2006). The teacher must gradually release the leadership role to learners, encourage cooperative learning and peer support amongst the learners. Reciprocal teaching is an approach that can assist learners from guided practice to gradually taking on responsibility and development and using strategies appropriately. During this process, the teacher monitors learners' use of the strategy, reminding them where necessary to apply the strategy, repeating much of the explanation from demonstration.

After some time, the teacher's support is reduced and learners progress to self-regulated learning. Learners take turns to lead the discussion about specific parts and applying the strategy. One learner serves as the discussion leader, asking questions about key ideas in the text, and other learners answer the questions and ask questions of their own. The learner leader helps the group clarify difficult words or passages that might hinder comprehension. Next, the leader summarises the text that had just been read and predicts what might come next. The process continues for each part of the text, with learners taking turns leading the discussion. In this way, learners are actively involved in their own learning.

Bruner's Theory of Learning and Development

Jerome Bruner (1986) developed a theory of cognitive development in which he maintained that thinking and reasoning are integrated into a single process. He stated that a child passes through several stages of development which he termed the inactive, iconic and symbolic modes. The inactive mode is seen in infants when they reach and grasp objects. In the iconic mode, the child will give meaning to previous experiences as he thinks about these experiences. The child then proceeds to the symbolic mode, which is regarded as the highest form of thinking wherein the child can attach names to objects or items in his surroundings because of his increased language ability (Mwamwenda, 1995:104-105). Bruner's theory advocates learning through discovery and active learning where the problem-solving skills of learners are encouraged. Bruner's theory is important for my research project. He regards human beings as primarily information processors, learners, thinkers, creators and storytellers (Bigge and Shermis, 1999:133). Like Piaget and Vygotsky, Bruner regards social and cultural factors as important in cognitive development (Driscoll, 1994:208). These aspects are relevant in the teaching of reading comprehension. Reading comprehension is the process of simultaneously extracting and constructing meaning (Snow and Sweet, 2003:1). This implies that the purpose of reading is to read the text with understanding.

The implications of this theory for teaching reading comprehension is that new concepts should be presented repeatedly, initially at a simple level and overtime at an increasingly difficult level, a concept Bruner referred to as the 'spiral ordering of content'. By applying this theory, the teacher is able to deal with important reading comprehension issues. A supportive environment will encourage learners to share information with their peers and to develop their problem-solving skills. Making use of problem-solving activities would also be a way of utilising Bruner's theory when teaching reading comprehension.

Ausubel's Cognitive Field Theory

For meaningful learning to occur learners must be ready and willing to relate new concepts to their current experience, and the new material should have the potential to be related to what the learner already knows. Meaningful learning occurs when learners actively process the information they are asked to learn. Ausubel (1963) refers to his theory as verbal learning, because most of what is learnt in the classroom is based on language as a means of communication, whereby learners are presented with all possible information on a given topic in its final form. Another concept of Ausubel (1963) is called 'reception learning', which means that learners receive information, think about it deductively and then apply this information. Ausubel believed that learning occurs because of the relatedness of what learners know and what they learn. Information is said to be meaningful if it can be related in some way to the learners' present, past or future experiences (Haas and Parkay, 1993:144).

Ausubel's theory has implications for teaching reading comprehension because teachers must be aware of the fact that certain minimal levels of intellectual maturity are necessary before various subjects can be taught with a reasonable degree of efficiency and with hope of success. Therefore, teachers must use the existing interests of learners, consider their point of view and take into account their limitations in the command of language and their grasp of concepts.

Bandura's Social Learning Theory

Bandura (1977) developed a social learning theory in which he postulated that children use rewards, punishment and imitation to understand the working of the world (Kail, 2001:459). According to Bandura (1977), the environment plays an important role in the child's life because this is where he or she interacts with other people who could provide important information about the world and act as role models to the child.

The child's interaction with other people is based on observing their norms, values and beliefs within the context of a particular society and the child is most likely to imitate adults with whom he or she has an emotional or nurturing bond which Bandura calls 'naturant models'. In his theory, Bandura (1977) refers to this concept as 'modelling', which means that learners learn positive or negative behaviour patterns from observing behaviour. When the learner interacts with people, he or she is being socialised and as a result, he or she adopts and lives according to what has been seen (Mwamwenda, 1995:203).

Another concept in Bandura's theory is that '...experience gives learners a sense of self-efficacy, which refers to learner's beliefs about their own abilities and talents' (Kail, 2001:16). This means that learners will have a good sense of what they can or cannot do and therefore will mostly not imitate the actions of someone if they feel their own abilities are not similar. The imitation of a model is important in a classroom situation; learners are expected to pay adequate attention to what the teacher says so that they can understand what is being taught. With memory, what is being observed must be processed into short-term and long-term memory for storage, so that it can be retrieved when such information is needed. Observation is important because the behaviour displayed by the model should be reproduced. For an observed behaviour to be reproduced perfectly, practice is important. Reinforcement also plays an important role and if modelled behaviour is rewarded, the chances of this behaviour being repeated are high (Hjelle and Ziegler, 1981:246-249; Engler, 1985:391-401).

This theory is very important for reading comprehension because learners imitate what they see other people doing, be it parents or teachers. Teachers are regarded as good models as they usually have positive and nurturing relationships with the learner. They should therefore display positive reading comprehension strategies so that learners can imitate and internalise these.

The above mentioned theories formed the foundation of Zimmerman's applied social-cognitive model of self-regulated learning. For example, for the learners to become independent readers who could master of their own learning they should be actively involved in their own learning, think independently, recall, analyze information and construct meaning from the text. Learners should gain confidence through regular practice which involve modelling.

Gardner's Theory of Multiple Intelligence

Gardner's theory of multiple intelligences is concerned with differences in the process of learning. In 1993, Gardner introduced his theory of multiple of intelligences. In his book, *Frames of Mind*, (1993) Gardner suggests that an individual does not only have a single intelligence. Rather than viewing intelligence as a single capacity, Gardner believes that in the existence of several intelligences (Brand and Donato, 2001:16). Gardner's theory puts emphasis on intelligence, these include psychometric, developmental, psychobiological and theories of multiple forms of intelligences. Each will be discussed briefly.

Psychometric Approach

This approach acknowledges a single, unitary and quantitative concept of intelligence. As it focuses only on linguistic and logical-methematical skills, the results are relatively easy to quantify.

Developmental Approach

A descriptive of how individuals develop progressively at different ages and continually shift between the assimilation of new information into existing cognitive structures forms the foundation of this approach (Teale, 2000:5). Theorists such as Piaget, Bruner and Vygotsky are strong supporters of this approach (Meyer and Van Ede, 1998:70-75).

Psychobiological Approach

This approach upholds a multifaceted theory of intelligence rather than a single factor theory. Cognitive functions occur in multiple, specific areas of the brain and are strongly influenced by the emotional centres of the brain. These functions are influenced by a combination of genetics, personal life experiences and situations (Gardner, 1993: 36-47).

Theories of multiple intelligence support the fact that individuals process information in multiple, interactive and complex ways (Teale, 2000:12). The focus is on individual differences among learners with the aim of promoting the fullest possible intellectual development of each one (Dryden and Vos, 1997:345; Lazear, 1994:191) to achieve this in teaching reading comprehension, teachers must employ a variety of strategies in order to assist learners to read the text with understanding. These theories acknowledge that there are many ways in which a person can be intelligent; as long as the opportunities will be available to activate the potentials. In the teaching of reading comprehension these potentials will or will not be activate provided, depending on the values of a particular culture, the opportunities that are available as well as decisions made by teachers, parents and the learners themselves. In this theory culture is important and can be regarded as a tool for learning and problem solving (Campbell, Campbell and Dickinson, 1999; xvi).

Gardner (1993:69) proposes that all individuals possess at least eight different intelligences, each with varied abilities. In the teaching of reading comprehension learners represent different was of learning. Therefore, the teachers' role is to provide opportunities for learners to learn. Therefore the aim of teaching reading comprehension is to teach the strategies in such a way that learners can understand the text and at the same time be able to use the strategy independently. This will maximise each learner's potential.

Gardner's theory suggests that there are eight intelligences' namely verbal-linguistic, logical-mathematical, visual-spatial, bodily-kinesthetic, musical-systemic, interpersonal, intrapersonal and naturalistic intelligences. Each has an influence in the teaching of reading comprehension.

Verbal-Linguistic

Verbal linguistic intelligence refers to the ability to use language (both spoken and written words, to express and appreciate complex meanings (Armstrong, 1994:2, Campbel *et al.,* 1999: xvi). Persons with this strength have a well developed auditory skills, enjoy reading and writing, like playing word games, spell accurately and use language fluently (Teale, 2000:28). Language is important in reading comprehension. Decoding enhance comprehension.

Logical-Mathematical

Logical-mathematical intelligence involves the capacity to

analyse problems logically, carry out intricate mathematical operations, investigate issues in a scientific way and consider propositions as well as hypotheses (Campbell *et al.,* 1999:xvi; Gardner, 1999a:42). Persons with this strength enjoy exploring patterns and relationships and making connections (Brand and Donato, 2001:18). Even though it is not mathematics, however, during reading comprehension, learners are required to retell or explain the events in the text logically for example, what happens first, secondly this are what happens.

Visual-Spatial Intelligence

Visual-spatial intelligence refers to the potential to recognise and manipulate patterns in both wide spaces as well as space more confined areas such as that used by surgeons, sculptors or artists (Gardner, 1999a:42). Individuals with this strength think best with the aid of pictures, images and graphic representations (Brand and Donato 2001:19, Teale, 2000:34, Drydon and Vos, 1997:344). As these people have an exceptional ability to think on a three dimensional level (Campbell *et al.*,1999: xvi), they enjoy completing jigsaw puzzles, doing map work and interpreting diagrams and charts. Also included is the ability to visualise something and thereafter, to graphically represents what was visualised. During reading comprehension learners use pictures to understand the text, for example, during prereading the teacher asked learners to predict about talk about the illustrations and make some predictions.

Bodily-kinesthetic: The core operations associated with bodily-kinesthetic intelligence include exceptional control over gross and fine motor actions as well as the ability to manipulate objects (Gardner *et al.,* 1996:209). People with this strength use their body, or certain parts thereof, in a skilled way (Gardner, 1999:42). This intelligence involves the ability to express emotions and thoughts through dance, mime, drama, charades and body language (Lazear, 1994:17). People with well developed gross-motor skills usually excel in games and sport (Teale, 2000:38-39). Many people with this strength are mechanically-minded and enjoy the use of manipulative. They learn best by participating in activities as they remember best what was done rather than what was observed or heard. During reading comprehension, both fiction and non-fiction are read. Figurative language and humor is used to compare movements of characters so that learners could understand the text.

Musical-rhythmic intelligence: A person's musical-rhythmic intelligence is one of the earliest to emerge (Brand and Donato, 2001:17). Those who excel in this area, portray exceptional skills in the performance, composition or appreciation of musical patterns (Gradner, 1999a:42). People with this strength create, communicate and understand meanings made out of sound, including environmental sounds (Armstrong, 1994:3; Gardner *et al.*, 1996:205). These people are extremely sensitive to the emotional power of music. During reading comprehension, language and vocabulary is important to assist learners to understand the text. Pictures are also important to assist learners to understand the text.

Interpersonal: As this intelligence involves learning through interaction with others (Brand and Donato, 2001:19; Campbell *et al.,* 1999: xvi), it is referred to as social intelligence (Dryden and Vos, 1997:350). It also refers to the skill of solving problems as a group and understanding another person's feelings, fears, motivations, intentions, desires, beliefs and anticipations (Gardner *et al.,* 1996:211: Lazear, 1994:19). During reading comprehension, learners read picture story books for example books that are presented in a dialogue form, fairy tales.

Intrapersonal: Self-knowledge and the ability to act adaptively on the basis of knowledge form the essence of intrapersonal intelligence (Gardner, 1999a: 43). Skills related to this intelligence include self-awareness, self-regulation, self-assessment, self-motivation as well as meatcognition (Brand and Donato 2001:19). During reading comprehension learners read books and stories from the past, use language to write their own bibliography.

Naturalistic: The essence of the naturalistic intelligence is the human ability to distinguish between a variety of species of fauna and floras well as making other distinctions in nature (Brand and Donato, 2001:20). People displaying this strength enjoy being outdoors, listening to sounds from the environment, classifying plants, minerals, rocks, grass and minerals. During reading comprehension learners read non-fiction stories, big books with various topics in nature, explaining simple facts, reading simple weather forecasts, stories from different cultures featuring animal characters and their traits or stories about sun, moon enrich this intelligence. Comprehension seems to be the reason for reading. For learners to read to learn they need to use problem-solving, thinking process the theory of multiple intelligences seems to be important in reading comprehension.

Conclusion

The purpose of theories is to bring form, coherence, and meaning to what we observe in the real world. Theories are helpful in sorting and evaluating the bewildering deluge of new materials, techniques, machines, gadgets, methods, and media confronting the educator.

Theories in this context are meant to be working statements. As John Dewey (1946:202) wrote, theories are not meant to be ideas "frozen into absolute standards masquerading as eternal truths" or "programmes rigidly adhered to". Rather, theory is to serve as a guide in systematising knowledge and as a working concept to be modified in the light of new knowledge. This process of theory building can be useful in separating what we know from what we believe it provides a guide for action, clarifies and structures, thought, and create for further research.

Osipow *et al.,* (1990:25) identify at least four ways in which learning theories may be helpful and useful in a learning situation. First, theory assists the teacher to plan strategy or treatment plan. Second, theory contributes to the understanding of human behaviour or, more specifically, of learner behaviour. Third, theory suggests certain learning techniques. Fourth, theory identifies goals and objectives to be pursued for learner benefit and evaluation.

Every discipline is dependent on the concepts and ideas contributed by earlier theorists. We build on the underlying support of past theories, even though we modify and change them. A theory can be challenged, modified, or strengthened as researchers and practitioners test its relevance and usefulness.

Chapter - 2

Teaching Reading

Introduction

A child's success at school and throughout life depends largely on the ability to read and understand the text. Rading involves individual's cognitive processes. It opens the door to personal freedom and if not achieved can shut the door to opportunities. It requires many basic processes such as identification of letters, mapping of letters onto sounds and the recognition of words and syntax. If learners experience difficulties in reading, it becomes difficult to excel in their schooling. Teachers, have the profound challenge of making reading a reality for all learners. A student's academic progress is profoundly shaped by the ability to understand what is read. Learners who cannot understand what they read, are not likely to acquire the skills necessary to participate in the 21st century workforce' (Butler, Urrutia, Buenger and Hunt, 2010:1).

Reading is a completely individual activity which takes place in all different ways from reading newspapers, magazines, written texts, telephone directories, labels on medicine bottles, etc. The ability to read is such a natural part of human beings that they seldom try to define reading. However, there are still different points of views on what reading is.

Reading is an essential skill for English as a second or foreign language (ESL/EFL). For many, reading is the most important skill to master. With strengthened reading skills, ESL/EFL readers will make greater development in all academic areas.

Definition

Reading has many definitions and the importance of reading in one's life cannot be underestimated. According to Nicholson (2000), reading is a multi-component process and improve writing Pretorious (2002). It involves decoding printed words into their linguistic forms, accessing the meanings of words, parsing of groups of words both in phrases and sentences. This can be semantically analysing sentences and putting the meaning of sentences to make up the text.

Reading is seen as a message-getting process; this process is often referred to as a 'metacognitive information process' which entails thinking about thinking (Clay,1993:10; Dorn and Soffos, 2005:37).

In their model of reading Luke and Freebody, (1999:5-8) identified four roles that effective readers need to learn to use. These are code-breakers, text participant, text-user and text analyst.

As code breakers the reader gives attention to letter-sound correspondences, whole words, sentences, paragraphs, semantic information, pronunciation and word meaning. In the role of text-participant the reader is concerned with what the text is saying in the context of the reader's own knowledge about the topic. Text-user practices refer to the way we use texts to achieve our particular social purpose. Text-analyst practices refer to the ways readers critique the underlying and unstated assumptions in text and the way a text attempts to position them as a reader.

"Reading not only educates the head but the heart as well. It promotes empathy and invites readers to adopt new perspectives. It offers opportunities for children to learn to recognise our similarities value our differences and respect our common humanity. In an important sense, then children need literature that serves as a window onto lives and experiences different from their own and literature that serve as a mirror reflecting themselves and their cultural values, attitudes and behaviours (Machado, 1999: 226)."

The most important task of the primary teachers is to develop readers and writers. Therefore, explicit teaching of the reading strategies can make learners to become competent readers. What determines the learners' progress in learning to read is his/her level of phonemic/phonological awareness and alphabetic knowledge. (Murray, 2006).

Children must be introduced to books and stories straight away, letting children play with books and discover what books and written language are about. Readers learn about written language while playing and working with real books (Flanagan, 1995:16).

Reading does not start at school; an important role is made by parents and caregivers to children's reading development.

Reading is a cognitive, social, emotional and cultural value. Taylor, Harris, Pearson and Garcia (1995:3-5) described reading as follows:

Language process and act of communication, because it is related to the other language processes which readers acquire: listening, speaking and writing.

Reading is one of the uniquely human and complex cognitive processes, because like the speaking process it is also related to other cognitive processes such as attribution of meaning, observation, perception and memory. This is because in order to read the child requires many basic processes; identification of letters, mapping of letters onto sounds and the recognition of words and syntax.

Socialisation process on various levels of communication with an absent writer or author who has an influence on the readers understanding and motivation (In addition, it often takes place in a social situation, such as a classroom or within a group. Even in the home it takes place in interaction with the learner's parents, friend and brothers and sisters. It enables readers to partake in a wide variety of social activities and prepares them to become part of a particular social group and to pursue a specific career).

Interactive process during which the reader, the text and the writer and the context in which the reading takes place, determine the nature and quality of the reader's comprehension, so that;-

The reader's background, experience, memory, motivation and so on.

The writer's ideas which have been transferred to writing and which are important in the writer's world.

The interaction between the reader and his or her friends and the teacher, the place where the reading takes place and the reason for reading are all involved.

Developmental Stages of Reading Development

There are three different stages of reading development. Teachers should be aware of these stages and assist learners to move from one stage to another competently.

Prereader

During the prereader stage the learner is expected to hold the book and turns pages correctly; recognise the beginning and the end of the page; listens and respond to stories; interpret the pictures; pretends to read loudly and silently; knows some letters and shows interest in print and pointing at them whenever they see signs and labels; create stories out of pictures.

Emergent Reader

The emergent readers uses pictures to tell story; knows some sounds and some letters that could make a sound; aware that reading starts from left to right; likes to join someone who is reading; recognise some words, and their names and some print in the environment, reads some familiar books.

Early Reader

Knows some letter sounds and names; recognise some common words; can retell a story; uses pictures to make meaning of the written text; reads alouds when reading to self; reads word for word loudly; reads early readers and picture books with pattern and repetition and rhyme.

The Developing Reader

Use pictures to make reading; use knowledge of sentence structure; use phonics to decode words; combines words into phrases; retells the beginning, the middle and the end of the story; can also give some details of the story; use punctuation marks; reads silently; corrects himself; reads books with large prints.

The Early Fluent Reader

Teachers can instill reading skill to make leaners an early fluent reader and to know how to read in the foundation phase. *Pacific Resources for Education and Learning (2012) state that Early fluent learners* are able to use several strategies to predict a word, often using pictures to confirm predictions. They can discuss the background of the story to better understand the actions in the story and the message the story carries. It is this time in the reader's development that the cueing systems are called upon significantly, so they must pay close attention to the visual cues and language patterns, and read for meaning in order to develop reading skills. It is a time when reading habits of risk-taking, and of predicting and confirming words while keeping the meaning in mind are established. At this stage, reading is more automatic, with more energy devoted to comprehension than word attack. Readers are approaching independence in comprehending text. Reading A-Z indicate that these readers are experiencing a greater variety of text and are able to recognize different styles and genres. Independence often varies with the type of text being read. Books at this stage have: More pages, Longer sentences, More text per page, Richer vocabulary, Greater variation in sentence pattern, Less reliance on pictures and More formal and descriptive language.

The Independent Reader

To achieve constructing of meaning form texts, learners should be able to use strategies while reading the text. It is important that reading strategies should be identified and practiced in classrooms. The strategies will help learners to construct meaning with ease. Reading strategies are behaviours which can be observed such as clarifying thinking in order to understand the text (Dorn and Soffos 2005:41). In essence teachers teach reading strategies by way of modelling, demonstrating and giving the necessary support. We can generate children's metacognitive awareness of these strategies and usefulness by naming the strategies, demonstrating them, and involving children in applying the strategies themselves (Weaver, 2002:331). In reality, to generate children's awareness of strategies, teachers teach for strategies. Clearly in the process teachers must support learners in developing a strategy system (Fountas and Pinnell, 1996:149). Teaching for reading strategies involves regular reading of texts in the classrooms.

Strategies//Techniques of Teaching Reading

- Educator models reading.
- Learners listen, respond, ask questions and make connections.
- During the reading, educator stops and "thinks aloud".

Shared Reading

- Shared reading involves a child and teacher or other adult reading together, in one-to-one interaction, from a book. It is practice frequently used in early year's classrooms and it is a practice commonly used by many parents at home. The single most important activity for building the knowledge and skills eventually required for reading appears to be reading aloud to children.

This is a lesson

- Explicit instruction how to use the text to support decoding and comprehension.
- Educator shares his/her thought processes to demonstrate how to integrate decoding and comprehension strategies.
- Learners practise strategies that they will use during guided reading.

Guided Reading

- Direct teaching of skills and strategies.
- Educator connects strategies taught, modelled and practised during read aloud and shared reading.
- Ideally, learners demonstrate strategies they have learnt from read aloud and shared reading lessons.
- Educator observes and determines what needs to be consolidated or revised during future read aloud and shared reading sessions.

During the guided reading educators do the following:

- Educator allows learners to take responsibility.

- S/he responds to learners' needs within each session.
- Lesson has less direct instruction and more talk about use of strategies.
- Learners read a lot.

Independent reading

- When reading alone, learners can independently apply what they have learnt throughout the scaffolding process.
- "Scaffolding toward independence is not about teachers knowing how to hold the readers up; it is about knowing how to let the readers go." (p.18)

The texts should be

- Should be "just challenging enough" (p. 37).
- In order to implement what they have learnt, learners need to read easier text.
- If text is too challenging, educator tends to do too much of the work.
- Learners need to be able to monitor their reading and problem solve independently.
- Need to give learners opportunities to think deeply!

Summary

- Reading and independent reading are connected and equally important.
- If learners cannot integrate decoding and comprehension smoothly, then the text is too hard.
- Decoding and comprehension are equally important right from Gr. R.
- A scaffolded, balanced approach to reading instruction facilitates successful independent reading.

Methods for Teaching Reading

There are various methods of teaching reading. There is no method that is the best. However, the most important aspect of teaching reading is that learners are taught by a research-based method of instruction that will introduce them to reading. Each method represents a certain beliefs about the processes involved in reading and the way in which learners acquire reading skills. Learners learn in different ways and so they differ in the type of methods they need to become proficient readers. It is, however, important for teachers to know them because they work both different learners who have their individual pace and rate of learning. Once learners are taught by these methods, the teacher will be able to identify the method of reading instruction the learner needs for greater success (Duffy, Anderson, Durham, Erickson, Guion, Ingram, 2003).

The Phonic Method

Phonics' is an educational term that refers to the myriad of methods used to teach the reader about correspondences between letters and sounds. Learners can learn phonics from an early age. It is a way of teaching children the relationship between phonemes and graphemes (sounds and symbols) to help them sound out words. There is a value in teaching learners sounds and symbols (Joubert, Meyer and Bester, 2008) especially at the beginning grades before grade 4.This method explicitly teaches the relationship between sounds and letters. It helps the learners to identify and sound new words both. Phonics instruction makes learners to read letters of the alphabet and to use them and to decode new words. Through this method learners can match the letters with the sound is called sound symbol association, because when learners know how to sound out letters, they can begin to put the sounds together to read simple words. learners can be able to sound out many words, even long and difficult words can be sounded out by learners from an early age.

- For children to be able to read they should go under the following stages;
- Be able to recognise sound, link sound and symbol, be able to sound out letter combinations of words, be able to blend and put together the individual sound.

Compare with the meaning emphasis of the whole language the phonics or skills-based approach is founded on the belief that a learner needs to be taught explicitly the component skills and strategies necessary for processing print. These skills include phonemic awareness, letter recognition, and all levels of phonic decoding, sound blending, and the identification of unknown words by analogy with known words (Westwood, 2001).

> "when phonics instruction is linked to children's reading and writing, they are more likely to become strategic and independent in their use of phonics than when phonics instruction is drilled and practised in isolation" (IRA, 1997, p. 2).

Hoffman and McCarthey (2000) have translated the principles of phonics instruction espoused by the IRA into the following operational terms. Phonics instruction should be:

- Explicit-not incidental;
- Pervasive-presented with a variety of contextualised reading and writing tasks;
- Systematic-building from simple skills in phonics to more complex letter clusters;
- Strategic-identifying when and how to use phonic decoding;
- Diagnosti-revealing what children already know and what they need to know.

However there is some problem identified in regard to phonics method. For example, learners can sound difficult words but are unable to comprehend what they read. In addition, phonics method may lead to learners' inability to spell words accurately. It is the comprehension, not word-calling that defines the complex process of learning to read (Jalongo,1998).

The Look and Say Method

Another method which can be used in teaching reading is the look and say method. According to Foertsch (2003:10), this approach is based on the premise that the easiest material for children to read is their own writing and that of their classmates. The stories that children themselves compose orally or in writing are the primary reading materials.

- In this method learners are taught to recognise the whole words or sentences rather than individual sounds. Learners look at a word which the teacher reads and in turn repeat the word. This is called the whole word approach to teaching reading. The method draws attention to a whole word rather than its phonetic elements. When using this method, the teacher picks words from the reading passage, reads the word and after reading them, writes them on flash cards, flash the word to the learners and the learners tell the teacher the words they have read on the flash cards and their meanings in order to learn with understanding. It is important to unpack the words in order for the learners to get the meaning of the words and understands the text. This is important for communication.

The Combined Approach

- In this method the teacher uses a combination of methods in order for the learners to master the reading skill. The teacher may use the phonic method as well as the look and say method in one lesson. In this way the teacher is able to attend to individual learners learning problems.

Whole Language Approach

Whole language is another method used to teach reading to young children.The whole language approach is rooted in Vygotsky's theory. It is important that teachers should have a knowledge base about theories because they can link with the methods of teaching. Whole language approach developed by Goodman (1986). 'It is not a dogma to be narrowly pactices, it is a way of bringing together a view of language, a view of learning, and a view of people, in particular groups of people: kids and teachers'(Goodman,1986:5). This method aims at a progressive, systematic acquisition of reading and writing skills. It has its roots in the principle that language can be learned thorough mastery of various easily identified skills thus making it learner centred (Chatry-Komarek, 2003:70).

Whole language theories explain the reading behaviour as something which must be allowed to grow within the child's already established, internalised rule system about oral language Kemp (1993). Whole language is a philosophy about learning to read and use language that emphasises the wholeness of the integrated language forms- oral language, reading and writing. Characteristics of the whole language view of learning to read are described by Goodman (1986, 1989,1990), who is a pioneer of the whole language movement:

- The whole language philosophy builds around whole learners, learning whole language in whole situations;
- Whole language learning encourages respect for language and for learners;
- Whole language instruction emphasises the meaning and not the language itself, in authentic speech and literacy events (Lerner, 1997:401).

There are many researchers in the area of reading, each as his own way of explaining about reading. However, they have common general principles which characterise 'whole language approach' (Goodman (1992), Watson (1989), Cambourne (1988) and Weaver (1994).

Readers construct meaning for themselves by drawing on clues, prior experience and personal purpose as they read. As they interact with print, readers predict, hypothesis, confirm and self-correct. Comprehension is the main purpose of readers.

Learning is enhanced when learners actively interact with other learners, books, materials and the world.

Learning is a social act. It supports exploration and taking risks.

Learning that is purposeful for the learner is more effective and enduring than that which is imposed by outside forces. When learners interested in a topic, they are more likely to take risks and to achieve success.

Literacy develops from whole to part and from known to unknown.

In this model the teacher fosters the language skills by tailoring them to the learners needs. This model puts emphasis on learners' cognitive development and it considers learning to read as a holistic, unitary process. Boyer (1996:9) says that reading cannot be taught in isolation but should be taught as part of the gestalt of literacy, which implies a holistic concept. In essence a holistic approach to language could, help the teacher to develop better readers and more literate citizens. The whole language approach is about constructing knowledge which emphasises knowing and developing the child's reading process (Chatry-Komarek, 2003:71). This model emphasis that reading is based on information that comes to the eye from the brain rather than information that comes to the eye from the printed page. Reading is a process of predicting meaning and sampling the print to confirm that prediction.

Goodman (1973) and his whole language philosophy: "Teach them to read for meaning and the words will fall into place" (p. 13). Some of the hallmarks of a whole language classroom included:

- Replacing basal readers with quality children's literature;
- Replacing direct instruction in phonetic word elements with a literacy rich environment, including print and authentic experiences with print;
- Minimising emphasis on accuracy of children's oral reading and emphasising meaning;
- Referring to oral "misreading" as "miscues"- indicators that the child has misread the cues for making meaning from print;
- Replacing formal testing with more "kid watching" (Manzo *et al.,* 2004, p. 179).

The assumption in the whole language approach is that children will learn rules naturally, without systematic instruction, by being immersed in a print-rich environment that invites guessing at words from context and from one's own experiential and conceptual knowledge. However, the student who does not crack the code with exposure to print requires systematic, explicit skill-by-skill phonics instruction to become proficient readers (Westwood, 2001). This does not preclude whole language instruction, as long as supplemental phonics is offered and the literature being read is appropriate to the student's language comprehension.

Characteristics of the whole language view of learning to read are described by Kenneth Goodman (1986, 1989 and 1990), who is a pioneer of the whole language movement:

- The whole language philosophy builds around whole learners, learning whole language in whole situations.
- Whole language learning encourages respect for language and for learners.
- Whole language instruction emphasises the meaning and not the language itself, in authentic speech and literacy events (Lerner, 1997, p. 401).

Through definitions may vary, there are general principles which characterise whole language. The following is a list builds from the works of Goodman (1992), Watson (1989), Cambourne (1988), Smith (1988) and Weaver (1994):

- Readers construct meaning for themselves by drawing on clues, prior experience and personal purposes as they read. As they interact with print, readers predict, hypothesise, confirm and self-correct. Comprehension is the primary goal of readers.
- Learning is enhanced when learners actively interact with other learners, books, materials and the world.
- Learning is a social act. It supports exploration and taking risks.
- Learning that is purposeful for the learner is more effective and enduring than that which is imposed by outside forces. When learners are interested in a topic, they are more likely to take risks and to achieve success.
- Literacy develops from whole to part and from known to unknown.

The main focus of whole language method is to teach learners to become competent, proficient in reading including fluency and comprehension and to be able to communicate what they have read through personal ideas, both orally and in written form. By employing whole language approach learners becomes exposed to many types of texts. They can use their prior knowledge and visual skills to help them read and understand the written text. This can enhance the writing skills in learners.

Models for Reading

Research indicates that reading is linked to meaning making from printed words (Clay,1993). Models are useful to teachers in that they give guidelines as to what methods are best employed in the teaching of reading.

These views are often grouped under three different reading models named the bottom up, the top-down and the interactive ones.

The Bottom-Up Approach

According to Dechant (1991), a bottom-up reading model is the model that emphasise the written or printed text; says reading is driven by a process that results in meaning (or, in other words, reading is driven by text), and proceeds from part to whole. A bottom-up reading model emphasises a single-direction, part-to-whole processing of a text.

In the beginning stages it gives little emphasis to the influences of the reader's world knowledge, contextual information, and other higher-order processing strategies (Dechant, 1991).

A bottom-up approach emphasise single direction, part to whole processing of a text, emphasises the written or printed text, says reading is driven by a process that results in meaning (reading is driven by text; and then proceeds from part to whole. This model works from bottom to top, that is it takes different elements of reading as its starting point and works towards the whole. It starts with print, then letter discrimination, blending of letters to form words. The child pronounces the word for meaning making. This model starts with the child's ability to recognise and decode letters, and then the reader progresses to larger units of print through the sentence up to the complete text (Wray and Medwell, 1997). Such models are also called outside in models because they make the assumption that reading is a process that begins outside the reader (Wray and Medwell, 1997:97). A phonic method of teaching reading is based on a bottom-up model. The belief which underpins it is that children must master individual components of reading first in order to be able to independently make meaning out of print.

According to the bottom-up model, reading was viewed as "the process of meaning interpretation" in which "the language is translated from one form of symbolic representation to another" (Nunan, 1991). It was also understood as the process of recognising the printed letters and words and building up a meaning from the smallest textual units at the bottom-up model (letter and words) to larger units at the top (phrases, clauses, intersentential linkages) (Rivers, 1964, 1968; Yorio, 1971). In other words, in the bottom-up model, the reader begins with the written text (the bottom) and constructs meaning from letters, words, phrases and sentences found within, and then processes the text in a linear fashion. Clearly, in the view of this driven model, the reader seems to play a relatively passive role because the basis of bottom-up processing is the linguistic knowledge of the reader.

Example

A widely accepted instructional programme that incorporates several bottom-up principles is the phonic approach to reading.

Features

Here are some features of a bottom-up approach to reading:

Bottom-up advocates believe the reader needs to

- identify letter features
- link these features to recognise letters
- combine letters to recognise spelling patterns
- link spelling patterns to recognise words, and
- then proceed to sentence, paragraph and text-level processing.

Top Down Model

This model starts with the child's past experience, prior knowledge as the basis for reading. It is thus learner centred. In other words, learners learn what they need to learn; seek the meaning of the words they sound. The model underpins holistic, whole book approaches to reading. In this model, reading was seen as the process in which readers move from the top, the higher level of mental stages down to the text itself. This approach emphasises the reconstruction of meaning rather than the decoding of form, the interaction between the reader and the text rather than the graphic forms of the printed pages. The readers proves his active role in the reading process by bringing to the interaction his/her available knowledge of the subject, knowledge of and expectation about how language works.

According to Ur (1996:138), "reading means reading and understanding" and according to Anderson (1991: 1) "reading is not a passive process but an active fluent process which involves the reader and the reading material in building meaning". What is more, meaning of the reading materials does not reside on the printed page, nor it is only in the head of the reader. A synergy occurs in reading which is the combination of the words on the printed page with the reader's background knowledge and experiences.

Apparently, the strong points of top-down model outnumber those of the bottom-up as the reader- the centre of the reading process- proves his active role. However, for some researchers, these models still reveal certain shortcomings. Stanovich (1988) stated that "the generation of hypotheses would actually be more time-consuming than decoding" and Eskey (1988: 93) believed that "in making the perfectly valid point that fluent reading is primarily a cognitive process, they (N.B: researchers who approved "in making the perfectly valid point that fluent reading is primarily a cognitive process, they (N.B: researchers who approved top-down models) tend to deemphasise the perceptual and decoding dimensions of that process".

Interactive Model

This model is underpinned by an interactive view of reading. Its starting point is developed from personal experiences of the learner and offers many opportunities for meaningful reading and writing activities. This model combines both top-down and bottom-up models of reading (Wray and Medwell,1991:100). The model claims that reading is both a cognitive and perceptual process in which the reader takes the responsibility of using his/her previous knowledge and experiences and codes the features of the text in order to make or establish meaning. Interactive theorists appreciate the role of prior knowledge and prediction, and at the same time emphasise the importance of rapid and accurate processing of the actual words of the text.

According to Hayes (1991: 7), "in interactive models, different processes are thought to be responsible for providing information obtained from each type of processing is combined to determine the most appropriate interpretation of the printed pages".

During guided reading teachers must:

- Teach in small groups;
- Match learners to instructional reading level;
- Use a common text;
- Give an introduction;
- Listen to learners read the text;
- Prompt, ask questions;
- Give instruction based on reading behaviour they notice;
- Support learners as they experiment with, develop and practise strategies to decode and understand text;
- Teach learners to support themselves rather than relying on someone else to support them;
- Use the balanced approach to reading in order to scaffold independent, meaningful reading.

Chapter - 3

Reading Comprehension Process

Introduction

Reading comprehension is a skill that is important in the educational success of learners. Without adequate reading comprehension skills, learners can struggle in many areas of their schooling and in life in general. Comprehension in reading is the ability to read and understand the written text. When learners comprehend a written passage, they construct meaning from the words to understand the passage as a whole. Learners can understand the text on various levels, identify simple facts from a passage (literal), make judgements regarding the passage's content (evaluative) and understand how the passage's content relates to other passages or to other situations (inferential level).

Why Is Comprehension Instruction Important?

Comprehension instruction is important because the concept of literacy is broadened of from literacy to 'literacies". Therefore, learners are facing an increased need for a high degree of literacy. We need to promote learners capacity to read and comprehend at all levels, literal, inferential and evaluative levels. There is a growing number of learners who cannot read and understand the text. As such policies and programmess are regularly adopted, but their efforts are uncertain (Rand report executive summary, 2002). It is critical that teachers must improve to promote reading comprehension skills in their teaching.

Definition

Shanahan (2006:28) defines reading comprehension as the act of understanding and interpreting the information with the text. This means that during reading comprehension, learners must be actively involved in order to construct meaning from the written text. Good reading comprehension involves reading the words on the page and accessing meanings. Thus, in order to understand the text, readers need to integrate the meanings of successive sentences and to establish local coherence. The interaction between the reader and the text becomes very important; and requires thoughtful interaction (Shanahan, 2006). The NRP (2000) describe reading comprehension as a result from a dynamic interaction of the words of the text at hand, the reader's purposes for reading, the reader's own prior knowledge of the world, language, and print and the comprehension strategies which the reader knows and employs to support understanding.

In their study, Kilfoil and Van der Walt (1997) raised the concern that quite often the teacher makes no effort to treat the comprehension text as a communication in which learners can develop the strategies that will enable them to make sense of comprehension text as communication. According to them, a typical reading comprehension lesson may follow the following steps:

- The teacher may explain or teach the vocabulary and then read the text aloud;
- The learners may then read the text silently alone;
- The teachers may go through the set question with the learners who may respond orally or by imitating and thereafter answers are checked.

However, Kilfoil and Van der Walt (1997:167) are against this method of reading and point out that the method has many weaknesses. For instance, the comprehension passage may not be a text that has been written primarily for its communicative value, but it might have been written to exemplify a single grammatical structure, and therefore may not be suitable for effective reading comprehension. This means that the question can be answered using the exact words of the passage, whereby the learners bypass any meaningful comprehension and merely depend on recognition of linguistic and lexical items that are common to other questions.

According to Cooper (2000), Duke and Pearson (2002), Marzano, Pickering and Pallack (2001) and Tompkins (2001), the reading comprehension lesson may follow various steps, namely:

- explanation, where the teachers explain to learners why the strategy helps comprehension;
- modelling, where the teacher models or demonstrate how to apply the strategy, usually by thinking aloud while reading a text;
- guided practice, where the teacher guides and assists learners as they learn how and when to apply the strategy;
- application, where the teacher helps learners to practise the strategy until they can apply it independently.

Shared Reading

Shared reading is an interactive process of reading. It involves the whole class. During this session, learners are required to read the key words and phrases they know and to teacher read aloud to the class. In a shared reading session, the teacher reads with the class or group using a large storybook that has big, bold print (DoE, 2008). Learners share the reading task with the teacher and gradually learners take over the task of reading (DoE, 2008). The purpose of shared reading is explained as follows: The teacher models reading strategies to learners using Big Books (Big books are large books with large illustrations and large print) and addressing specific skills in reading. During the lesson, the teacher leads a discussion of the cover and some of the illustrations in the book to place the text within the context of learners' prior knowledge, and encourages learners to predict what will happen in the story. The teacher reads using a pointer to point at the words as she/he reads. After reading, the teacher checks the learners' understanding of the text through discussion or questions. The benefits of shared reading are that the teacher models different reading comprehension strategies for the learners. The planned activities should cater for different learners' abilities by allowing them to join in wherever they can and the environment must be non-threatening for learners to experience success. During shared reading the teacher is expected to teach learners while they read certain kinds of texts, how they read the text, the expression and intonation (tone of voice) suited to the text, how to respond to the text; the text level, word level or sentence level features in the text and model. The teacher is expected to teach a variety of reading strategies and promote comprehension through differentiated questioning and discussion (DoE, 2008).

Group Guided Reading

Group guided reading is regarded as one of the key components of a balanced language programme (Hornsby, 2000; Cunningham and Alington, 1999; Pressley, 2002) and is a teacher-directed activity (DoE, 2008). It is an approach in which the teacher provides the structure and purpose of reading, and for responding to the material read. It involves using carefully selected books at the learners' instructional level. In group guided sessions, the learners can be grouped according to their reading abilities. The benefits are that it gives the teacher the opportunity to observe reading behaviours, identify areas of need and allow learners to develop more independence and confidence as they practice and consolidate reading behaviours and skills. During the process, the role of the teacher is to bring learners to a higher level by demonstrating, modelling, explaining and encouraging learners during reading (Opitz and Ford, 2001). The steps of the guided reading can be linked to the theory of Bruner's scaffolding process leading to independence. Teachers prepare ahead of time. Before reading starts, the teacher has to spend some time talking about comprehension strategies, introducing difficult words that are contained in the text and assisting individual learners to practice strategies for comprehending the text (Fountas and Pinnel, 2001). It provides opportunities for the teacher to integrate learners' growing knowledge of the conventions of print, letter-sound relationships and other foundational skills in context.

During guided reading learners are exposed to reading aloud and shared reading. Simultaneously, the teacher is able to teach learners how to construct meaning from the text by using strategies to self-pace, self-direct and self-monitor under the teacher's guidance. This kind of support is linked to Vygotsky's (1978; 1986) view that learners learn more as they get support from knowledgeable others. The South African government regarded it as the solution to the low level of literacy. However, according to a study on an evaluation of guided reading in three primary schools in the Western Cape, Kruizinga (2010) found that teachers had a superficial understanding of guided reading and that it was difficult for teachers to implement the steps for guided reading in their classrooms. However, the purpose of guided reading is to assist learners to become independent readers who can read the text for enjoyment and be able to get the meaning from the text.

Independent Reading

Independent reading is important in reading comprehension. During this activity, learners learn to apply the comprehension strategies independently that they were taught during guided reading (Biddulph, 2000). According to DoE (2008), independent reading is a purposeful planned activity. The teacher has a structured daily time during which learners associate themselves with books. Learners choose their own books according to their own interest and ability. However, learners should be guided to choose the texts that they can read with a high degree of success. During this session, the teacher should listen, observe and gather information about learners' reading behaviour. Learners are able to listen to themselves as they read and cross-check while they practice the strategies (Fountas and Pinnell, 1999). Fountas and Pinnell (1996) and Zimmerman (1998) support the view that learners learn best when they are responsible for their own learning. The goal of teaching reading comprehension strategies is for the learners to become self-managed readers who can take over the process themselves. However, Taberski (2000) argued that during independent reading, frustrated learners do not sustain their reading long enough to practice the skill. This is because they are unable to decode the words and do not understand the text. Therefore, independent reading could become a meaningless exercise.

Reading Aloud

Reading aloud is another approach that can have a positive effect on the development of reading comprehension (Lane and Wright, 2007). Read-aloud times should be a well-planned activity and not impromptu (Sipe, 2008). The teacher selects a book with repetitive texts and illustrations at a level that matches learners reading ability. Gradually, the selection should be to a level just beyond what learners can read independently to expand learners' engagement in print. The teacher should be well prepared, read to the whole class or to a small group, using material that is at the listening comprehension level of the learners (Teale, 2003). Reading aloud is regarded as the best motivator for instilling the desire to read in learners. In read-aloud sessions, the teacher reads to the whole class or to small group using material that is at listening comprehension level of the learners. The benefit of this approach to the learners is that it helps them to develop a love of literature, motivates them to read various kinds of texts on their own and increases their vocabulary (Lane and Wright, 2007). The speaking skills of the learners are enhanced by hearing good pronunciation and language use, as well as their thinking skills through their comprehension of the text and experience with cause and effect including logical sequencing.

According to the DoE (2008), reading aloud should occur every day to stimulate learners' interest in the written text. Several key activities take place before, during and after reading. With regard to the teaching of reading comprehension, the DoE (2008) emphasised that teachers should keep a close check on learners to ensure that they are not barking at print, but reading with understanding. They must also be able to and interpret what they read in various situations. Involving learners interactively while reading aloud help to improve comprehension whereas after-reading discussions encourage learners to link the story events to their personal experiences (Sipe, 2008). The teachers' handbook *Teaching reading in early grades* briefly explains to the teacher how to develop comprehension, but does not explain how comprehension should be taught and which strategies to use before, during and after reading in a Home Language classroom; therefore, there are no clear guidelines in the teachers' handbook about the teaching of reading comprehension to Tshivenda-speaking learners. Heugh (2005) concurs, stating that 'while the teachers' handbook for teaching reading in English has been developed and widely distributed across South African schools, the DoE has still not published one handbook for teaching reading in any other African languages'. Therefore, there is a need for guidelines to be developed to assist the African languages teachers in the languages they understand and with examples that they can use in their teaching.

Comprehension is the goal of reading and listening. We do it every day, often without being aware that we are doing it. However, the reader needs comprehension strategies in order to accomplish the task of reading most effectively, efficiently and meaningfully. Reading comprehension seems to be a complex process. Successful comprehension enables readers to acquire information, to experience and be aware of other worlds, to communicate successfully and to achieve academic success.

Goals of Reading Comprehension

In schools, reading comprehension has become a major priority. It is generally acknowledged that primary education is crucial stage in the life of a learner, because learning and developing reading comprehension skills are essential for learners throughout schooling. It is crucial that teachers should be competent to teach learners reading comprehension strategies. By the end of Grade 3 learners should be able to read, and read the text with understanding. All further learning rests on these foundations, which should enable learners to reach their full potential and function effectively in the society.

Comprehension is the reason for reading. If readers can identify the words but do not understand what they are reading, they have not achieved the goal of reading comprehension. To gain a good understanding of the text, children must bring to it the foundational knowledge and skills of oral language, prior knowledge experiences, concepts about print, phonemic awareness, letter-sound relationships, vocabulary and semantics and syntax. They must integrate what they bring to the text with the text itself.

The aim of teaching reading is to comprehend the text and be able to use the information in various situations (Sweet and Snow, 2002). Therefore, it is of utmost importance that teachers should use strategies that will enable learners to interact communicatively with a variety of written texts.

Comprehension is the sole reason for reading. If readers can read the words but do not understand what they are reading, one would hesitate to call that reading. It is therefore important that learners should understand what they read, be able to remember what they read and communicate with others about what they read.

Comprehension is the process of deriving meaning from the written text and to make use of the information in different situations. So the goal of teaching reading strategies is to help learners to comprehend text. Through this process learners develop the knowledge, skills, and strategies they must possess to become proficient and independent readers.

Pressely and Wharton-McDonald (1997:448) note that "there is abroad-base agreement that the most important goal of reading education is to develop readers who can derive meaning from texts". These are readers who will read the written text, understand it and use the information in different situations. Therefore, effective early reading instruction enables all children to become fluent readers who comprehend what they are reading, can apply and communicate their knowledge and skills in new contexts, and have a strong motivation to read.

It is clear that teachers should know the goals of reading instruction. The National Reading Panel (2003:13) Ontario identified three main goals for reading instruction:

- *Fluency is the ability to identify words accurately and read a text quickly with good expression. Fluency comes from practice in reading easy books about familiar subjects. These texts primarily contain familiar, high frequency words so that the child will encounter few unfamiliar words. As children develop fluency, they improve their ability to read more expressively, with proper phrasing, thus gaining more of the text's meaning.*

Comprehension is the ability to understand, reflect on, and learn from text. Too ensure that children develop comprehension skills, effective reading instruction builds on their prior knowledge and experience, language skills, and higher level thinking.

Motivation to read is the essential element for actively engaging children in the reading process. It is the fuel that lights the fire and keeps burning. Children need to be immersed in a literacy rich environment, filled with books, poems, pictures, charts, and other resources that capture their interest and make them want to read for information and pleasure.

The three goals are interconnected and that the strategies for achieving them work together synergistically (NRP: 2003, Ontario).

Comprehension reading instruction teaches the child to use a variety of skills to decode, read fluently and understand the text. However, although decades of research have revealed a great deal of information about how readers get meaning from what they read and about the kinds of explicit instruction and activities that are most successful in helping students to become good readers, recent classroom observation studies indicate that students in typical elementary school classrooms still receive little in the way of effective comprehension instruction (Pressley, 2000, Pressley,Wharton-McDonald, Hampson and Echevarria, 1998; RAND Reading Study Group, 2002).

In the same vein, Muspratt, Luke and Freebody, (1997) maintained that less research has been conducted on young learners' comprehension and that even the youngest readers' need opportunities to be code breakers, meaning makers, text users and text critics.

It is, therefore, important that before the reading comprehension activity, teachers should know and model effective comprehension strategies to the learners before, during and after reading; to help learners to arrive at a deeper understanding of what they read. Researchers Lehr and Osborn (2005:17) confirmed that for learners in Grade 3 and up, instruction in specific cognitive strategies can improve reading comprehension for all learners including poor readers. Therefore, what remains a challenge for teachers are what strategies to teach before, during and after reading and how to teach them (Armbruster, Lehr, and Osborn, 2001).

Five Essential Components of Effective Reading Instruction

The NRP Report (2000) identified five essential components of effective reading instruction, namely phonemic awareness, phonics instruction, fluency instruction, vocabulary instruction and text comprehension instruction. Of those five, text comprehension instruction was described as critically important in the development of learners' reading skills, the ability for learners to obtain education and the ability for persons to learn throughout life (NRP, 2000). The NRP report further indicated that comprehension skills should be developed through explicit instruction and practice in comprehension strategies. Deriving meaning from text can be extremely difficult process for children, adolescents and adults. The present study focuses on the teaching of reading comprehension to Grade 3 learners before reading, during reading and after reading.

Duffy and McIntyre (1982) made a similar observation with the primary teachers from grade one to six. A similar concern was raised by Kilfoil and Van der Walt (1997), McLaughlin and Allen (2002) who state that quite often the teacher makes no effort to treat the comprehension text as a communication in which learners can develop the strategies that will enable them to make sense of comprehension text as communication. Again, in their fourth and fifth grade classroom observation study, Pressley (2001), commented that he saw little comprehension instruction; and that teachers relied on post-reading comprehension questions. Pressley suggested that comprehension instruction is an important area of inquiry of reading and that there is a real need for many teachers to be aware of comprehension strategies before, during and after reading.

According to McLaughlin and Allen (2002) learners must be able to connect relevant prior knowledge to what they read, select valid thinking processes, construct mental images, question, infer, summarise, monitor whether or not they are understanding and eliminate confusions.

According to them a typical reading comprehension lesson may follow the following steps:

(a) The teacher may explain or teach the vocabulary and then read the text aloud.

(b) The learners may then read the text silently.

(c) The teachers may go through the set question with the learners who may respond orally or imitating then the answers is checked (Kilfoil *et al.,* 1977:167).

Therefore, the teaching of reading should focus on the instruction of strategies that will enable learners to acquire the skills that are necessary for effective communication.

Reading comprehension is a skill necessary to succeed in educational and vocational settings and to participate in society. Yet learners' reading comprehension abilities are often alarmingly low. Improving learners' reading comprehension abilities therefore is a very important task. Hence an investigation into the teaching of reading comprehension to Tshivenda-speaking Grade 3 learners.

The following section will discuss about the various models for reading comprehension as discussed by various researchers.

The Models of Teaching Reading Comprehension

There are many models of reading comprehension. To clarify how comprehension works, Pardo, (2004) give a detailed visual model of comprehension. Research shows that reading comprehension is linked with making meaning from printed words. The following models represent different views on how comprehension can take place (Pardo (2004), RAND Study Group (2000) and Pearson and Raphael (1990).

The first to discuss will be Pardos, (2004) model of comprehension

In this study the quote of Pardo, (2004:272) apply:

Once teachers understand what is involved in comprehending and how the factors of reader, text, and context interact to create meaning, they can more easily teach their students to be effective comprehenders.

That there is a great need to know just how much of an impact on reading achievement can be made by instruction, rich in all the individual components that increase comprehension. Of course, the hope is that there will be much benefit; the fear is that such instruction might be so overwhelmingly complex. If all the components are simply thrown into the mix, instruction will be confusing and effective. With some experience in a attempting to mix the components, how to create more effective teaching occurs. There is much interesting work ahead before comprehension instruction is understood fully.

The following is a visual representation of this model according to Pardo, (2004:272).

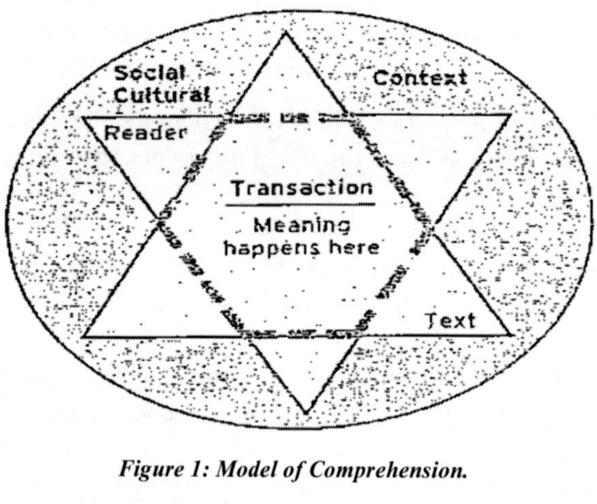

Figure 1: Model of Comprehension.

Pardo's (2004; 272) Visual Model of Comprehension

Pardo (2004) indicated that during reading comprehension, the reader brings many things to the literacy event. To clarify how comprehension works, Pardo (2004) give a detailed visual model of comprehension. According to Pardo (2004), comprehension processes may occur in different elements namely, reader, text, context and transaction (see the visual representation of comprehension below).

Pardo (2004) indicated that during reading comprehension, the reader brings many things to the literacy event. In each element, this model also gives details on how the teacher can interact with the model to help learners become strong comprehenders.

The above model suggests that comprehension processes may occur in different elements namely, reader, text, context and transaction. In each element, this model also gives details on how the teacher can interact with the model to help learners become strong comprehenders. Each of the elements will be discussed below:

The Reader

The model described that each reader comes to the reading process with his or her unique traits or characteristics that are distinctly applied with each text situation. So this means that each text requires specific strategies to use. Out of these traits the most important is the reader's world knowledge. The more background knowledge a reader has that connects with the text being read, the more likely the reader will be able to make sense of what is being read (Butcher and Kintsch, 2003; Schallert and Martin, 2003).

Pardo (2004) indicated that the amount and depth of a reader's world knowledge vary as do other individuals characteristics. Readers vary in the skills, knowledge, cognitive development, culture, and purpose they bring to the text (Narvaez, 2002). Skills include such things as basic language ability, decoding skills, and higher level thinking skills. Knowledge includes background knowledge about content and text and relates to the available schema a reader has for a particular text. A reader's cognitive development causes that reader to evaluate text in different ways for example, to make moral judgements.

Pardo (2004) further explains that comprehension is affected by a reader's culture, based on the degree to which it matches with the writer's culture espoused in the text. Another individual difference that exists in readers is motivation. Motivation can influence the interest, purpose, emotion, or persistence with which a reader engages with text (read (Butcher and Kintsch, 2003; Schallert and Martin, 2003). More motivated readers are likely to apply more strategies and work harder at building meaning. Less motivated readers are not likely to work hard, and the meaning they create will not be as powerful as if they were highly motivated.

Teachers Support Readers

The model explained how teachers can best support foundation phase learners to become competent comprehenders. Pardo, (2004) suggested that teachers must teach decoding skills, help students build fluency, build and activate background knowledge, teach vocabulary words, motivate students, and engage them in personal responses.

Each will be Discussed Below

Teach Decoding Skills

In order to comprehend, readers must be able to read words. Teachers must help learners to get to the level of automatic decoding by providing instruction in phonemic awareness and phonics at all grade levels.

Help Learners Build Fluency

According to Rasinski (2003), if learners becomes automatic, learners become fluent and can focus on comprehension. Teacher helps learners become more fluent by engaging them in repeated readings for real purpose.

Teacher must also model fluent reading by reading aloud to learners daily by reading aloud to learners daily so that they realise what fluent reading sounds like.

Build and Activate Prior Knowledge

Background knowledge is an important factor for creating meaning.

Teachers must help learners activate prior knowledge before reading so that information connected with concepts or topics in the text is more accessible during reading (Keen and Zimmermann, 1997; Miller, 2002).

Duke (2003) maintained that one way to add to the world of knowledge is to use informational books with all learners. This will later help learners to be able to activate information. Teacher must also support learners' acquisition of world knowledge by establishing and maintaining a rich, literate environment, full of texts that provide learners enormous opportunities to learn content in a variety of topics.

Teachers must create visual or graphic organisers that help learners see not only new concepts but also how previously known concepts are related and connected to the new ones (Keen and Zimmermann, 1997; Miller, 2002). Teachers teach learners how to make text-to-text, text-to-self, and text-to-world connections so that readers can more easily comprehend the text they read.

Reading aloud and modelling show learners how to activate schema and connections.

Teach Vocabulary Words

If there are too many words that a reader does not know, he or she will have to spend too much mental energy figuring out the unknown word (and will not be able to understand a passage as a whole. Teachers help learners learn important vocabulary words prior to reading difficult and unfamiliar texts. When teaching vocabulary words, teachers make sure that the selected words are necessary for making meaning with the text learners will be reading and that they help learners connect the new words to something they already know.

Motivate Learners

Provide learners with interesting texts, allowing them choices in reading and writing, and helping learners set authentic purposes for reading for example generating reports, writing letters, demonstrating some new ability or skill (Pressley and Hilden, 2002).

Engage Learners in Personal Response to Text

Teachers must help learners to learn and apply comprehension strategies while reading through writing, and during learners-led discussion groups called Book clubs, where learners explore the individual meanings that have emerged as they engage with the text over a period of time.

The Text

Understanding the reader is one important piece of the comprehension puzzle, but features of the text also influence the transaction where comprehension happens (Pardo, 2004). The structure of the text, its genre, vocabulary, language, even specific word choices-works to make each text unique. The content of the text, the difficulty or readability of it, and even the type of font and size are factors of a text that can influence readers interaction. Studies, Tracey and Marrow (2002) have shown that the quality of the text at the surface level is important for readers to be able to make meaning effectively.

Teachers Support Texts

Teacher helps learners to understand those features so they can comprehend effectively. Teachers teach text structures, model appropriate text selection, and provide regular independent reading time.

Teach Text Structures

Teachers select texts that have obvious structure. They teach a variety of narrative genres and some expository text structures. They teach specific elements that make each genre unique, for example, talking animals in a folk tales. This will, in a way help learners to access schema for a certain narrative genre when they begin to read a new text and can begin to make text to text connections for a particular story genre, which will help them more easily make meaning. Teachers share one common expository text structures with learners, such as sequence, description, comparison, and cause and effect. Teachers discuss the idea on inconsiderate texts (Armbruster, Lehr, and Osborn, 2001). With learners and show them how to use cues when reading nonfiction such as reading tables, charts, graphs, and the captions under pictures; using bold print and italics to determine bog or important ideas.

Model Appropriate Text Selection

Teachers teach learners how to select appropriate texts by showing them what features to consider; and must support learners throughout the year with appropriate book selection.

Provide Regular Independent Reading Time

Teacher can make sure they provide learners with time to read independently every day. Reading becomes better with practice, and comprehending becomes better with more reading practice (Pressley, 2003).

Teachers Create and Support a Socio-cultural Context

The model shows that reading takes place somewhere between a specific reader and a specific text. A socio-cultural influence likely to permeates any reading activity (Kucer, 2001; Schallert and Martin, 2003) depending on the place, the situation, and the purpose for reading, the reader and the text interact in ways that are unique for that specific context. The same reading at another time or in a different place might result in a different meaning. The context also involves the activity that occurs around the transaction. For example, if the teacher asks learners to read a particular text, the transaction that occurs will be based on this context. Teachers create contexts and learning opportunities that will support the construction of meaning.

According to Keene and Zimmermann (1997); Miller (2002) and Pardo (2002), environments that value reading and writing, that contain a wide variety of texts, that allow learners at risks and that find time for reading aloud and reading independently are contexts that promote effectively the construction of meaning of the text.

The Transaction

During the interaction between the reader, the text and the activity, the reader exits the transaction maintaining a mental representation or gist of the text. One way is by making inferences Readers are searching for coherence and for a chain of related events that can lead them to infer or make meaning.

As readers continue moving through the text, they continue to build inferences, drawing from long-term memory specific ideas that seem to create coherence and answer the question posed earlier. Inferencing, according to Butcher and Kitsch (2003) is one of the most important processes that occur during comprehension.

The next to be discussed will be a heuristic for thinking about reading comprehension- the RAND Reading Study Group Model (2002).

A Heuristic for Thinking About Reading Comprehension: The RAND Reading Study Group Model (RRSG, Snow, C, (2002)

In their definition, the RRSG (2002) define reading comprehension as the process of simultaneously extracting and constructing meaning through interaction and involvement with written language. The RRSG used the words *extracting* and *constructing* to emphasise both the importance and the insufficiency of the text as a determinant of reading comprehension.

They indicated that comprehension entails three elements namely, the *reader* who is doing the comprehending, the *text* that is to be comprehended and the *activity* in which comprehension is a part. The following graphic diagram represents the A Heuristic for Thinking About Reading Comprehension: The RAND Reading Study Group Model.

A Heuristic for Thinking About Reading Comprehension:

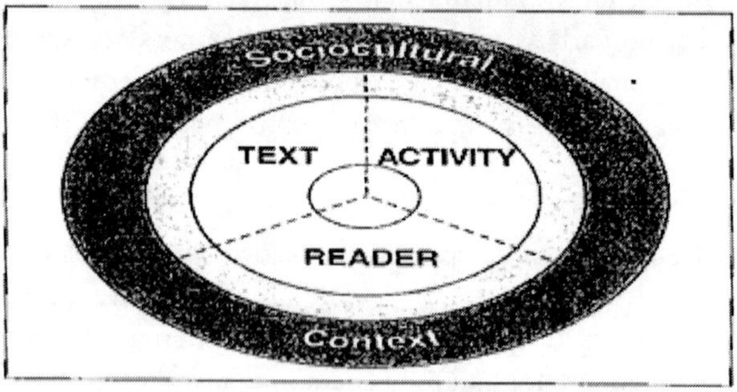

The RAND Reading Study Group Model (Snow, 2002).

In considering the reader, the RRSG included all the capacities, abilities, knowledge, and experiences that a person brings to the act of reading. They further explained that text is broadly construed to include any printed text or electronic text. In considering activity, they include the purposes, processes, and consequences associated with the act of reading.

According to Snow (2002), all three dimensions define a phenomenon that occurs within a larger socio-cultural context (see Figure) that shapes and is shaped by the reader and that interacts with each of the three elements. The identities and capacities of readers, the texts that are available and valued, and the activities in which readers are engaged with those texts are all influenced by, and in some cases determined by, the socio-cultural context. The socio-cultural context mediates students' experiences, just as students' experiences influence the context. I will elaborate on each element in subsequent sections.

Snow (2002) pointed out that reader, text, and activity are also interrelated in dynamic ways that vary across pre-reading, reading, and post-reading.

According to Snow (2002), each act of reading is potentially a micro developmental process. For example, in the prereading micro period, the reader arrives with a host of characteristics, including cognitive, motivational, language, and non-linguistic capabilities, along with a particular level of fluency.

During the reading micro period, some of these reader characteristics may change. Likewise, during the post-reading micro period of the same reading event, some of these same reader characteristics, or reading comprehension has focused on specific factors (e.g., vocabulary knowledge) without specifying either that the effect of that factor reflects a relationship among reader, text, and activity or that the factor may change from pre-reading to reading to post-reading.

The second element to be discussed will be the reader.

The Reader

To comprehend, a reader must have a wide range of capacities and abilities.

These include cognitive capacities (e.g., attention, memory, critical analytic ability, inferencing, visualisation ability), motivation (a purpose for reading, an interest in the content being read, self-efficacy as a reader), and various types of knowledge (vocabulary, domain and topic knowledge, linguistic and discourse knowledge, knowledge of specific comprehension strategies).

The specific cognitive, motivational, and linguistic capacities and the knowledge base called on in any act of reading comprehension depend on the texts in use and the specific activity in which one is engaged.

Fluency can be conceptualised as both an antecedent to and a consequence of comprehension. Some aspects of fluent, expressive reading may depend on a thorough understanding of a text. However, some components of fluency—quick and efficient recognition of words and at least some aspects of syntactic parsing-appear to be prerequisites for comprehension.

As a reader begins to read and completes whatever activity is at hand, some of the knowledge and capabilities of the reader change. For example, a reader might increase domain knowledge during reading. Similarly, vocabulary, linguistic, or discourse knowledge might increase. Fluency could also increase as a function of the additional practice in reading. Motivational factors, such as self concept or interest in the topic, might change in either a positive or a negative direction during a successful or an unsuccessful reading experience.

Another important source of changes in knowledge and capacities is the instruction that a reader receives. Appropriate instruction will foster reading comprehension, which is defined in two ways—the comprehension of the text under current consideration and comprehension capacities more generally.

Thus, although teachers may focus their content area instruction on helping learners understand the material, an important concurrent goal is helping learners learn how to become self-regulated, active readers who have a variety of strategies to help them comprehend.

Effective teachers incorporate both goals into their comprehension instruction. They have a clear understanding of which learners need which type of instruction for which texts, and they give learners the instruction they need to meet both short-term and long-term comprehension goals.

The next element to be discussed will be the text.

The Text

The features of text have a large effect on comprehension. Comprehension does not occur by simply extracting meaning from text. During reading, the reader constructs different representations of the text that are important for comprehension. These representations include, for example, the surface code (the exact wording of the text), the text base (idea units representing the meaning), and a representation of the mental models embedded in the text. The proliferation of computers and electronic text has led us to broaden the definition of text to include electronic text and multimedia documents in addition to conventional print. Electronic text can present particular challenges to comprehension, such as dealing with the non-linear nature of hypertext, but it also offers the potential for supporting the comprehension of complex texts, for example, through hyperlinks to definitions or translations of difficult words or to paraphrasing of complex sentences.

Texts can be difficult or easy, depending on factors inherent in the text, on the relationship between the text and the knowledge and abilities of the reader, and on the activities in which the reader is engaged. For example, the content presented in the text has a critical bearing on reading comprehension. A reader's domain knowledge interacts with the content of the text in comprehension. In addition to content, the vocabulary load of the text and its linguistic structure, discourse style, and genre also interact with the reader's knowledge. When too many of these factors are not matched to a reader's knowledge and experience, the text may be too difficult for optimal comprehension to occur. Further, various activities are better suited to some texts than to others. For example, electronic texts that are the product of Internet searches typically need to be scanned for relevance and for reliability, unlike assigned texts that are meant to be studied more deeply. Electronic texts that incorporate hyperlinks and hypermedia introduce some complications in defining comprehension because they require skills and abilities beyond those required for the comprehension of conventional, linear print.

The challenge of teaching reading comprehension is heightened in the current educational era because all learners are expected to read more text and more complex texts. Schools can no longer track learners so that only those with highly developed reading skills take the more reading-intensive courses.

The next element to be discussed will be the text.

The Activity

Reading does not occur in a vacuum. It is done for a purpose, to achieve some end. Activity refers to this dimension of reading. A reading activity involves one or more purposes, some operations to process the text at hand, and the consequences of performing the activity. Prior to reading, a reader has a purpose, which can be either externally imposed (e.g., completing a class assignment) or internally generated (wanting to program a VCR). The purpose is influenced by a cluster of motivational variables, including interest and prior knowledge.

The initial purposes can change as the reader reads. That is, a reader might encounter information that raises new questions that make the original purpose either incomplete or irrelevant. When the purpose is externally mandated, as in instruction, the reader might accept the purpose and complete the activity; for example, if the assignment is "read a paragraph in order to write a summary," the compliant student will accept that purpose and engage in reading operations designed to address it. If the reader does not fully accept the mandated purpose, internally generated purposes may conflict with the externally mandated purpose. Such conflicts may lead to incomplete comprehension. For example, if students fail to see the relevance of an assignment, they may not read purposively, thus compromising their comprehension of the text.

During reading, the reader processes the text with regard to the purpose. Processing the text involves, beyond decoding, higher-level linguistic and semantic processing and monitoring. Each process is more or less important in different types of reading, including skimming (getting only the gist of text) and studying (reading text with the intent of retaining the information for a period of time).

In a way, the consequences of reading are part of the activity. Some reading activities lead to an increase in the *knowledge* a reader has. Another consequence of reading activities is finding out how to do something. These *application* consequences are often related to the goal of the reader. Reading activities have *engagement* as their consequences. Good comprehenders can be engaged in many different types of text.

Knowledge, application, and engagement can be viewed as direct consequences of the reading activity. Activities may also have other, longer-term consequences. Any knowledge (or application) acquired during reading for enjoyment also becomes part of the knowledge that a reader brings to the next reading experience.

The next element to be discussed will be the context.

The Context

One important set of reading activities occurs in the context of instruction.

Understanding how the reader's purpose for reading and operations are shaped by instruction, and how short- and long-term consequences are influenced by instruction, constitutes a major issue within the research agenda we propose.

When we think about the context of learning to read, we think mostly of classrooms.

Children bring to their classrooms vastly varying capacities and understandings about reading, which are in turn influenced, or in some cases determined, by their experiences in their homes and neighbourhoods.

Further, classrooms and schools themselves reflect the neighbourhood context and the economic disparities of the larger society. The differences in instruction and in the availability of texts, computers, and other instructional resources between schools serving low-income neighbourhoods and those serving middle income neighbourhoods are well documented.

Sociocultural and sociohistorical theories of learning and literacy describe how children acquire literacy through social interactions with more expert peers and adults.

According to Vygotsky (1978), with the guidance and support of an expert, children are able to perform tasks that are slightly beyond their own independent knowledge and capability. Therefore, the nature of good learning emanate from Vygotsky's theory on social constructivism. Through social interactions and the opportunity to engage in increased practice, rehearsal, learners develop a profound understanding of the strategies underlying reading comprehension. Research (Rogoff, 1990) has revealed that adults in position of authority can play a major role in determining learner's ways of coping with a learning situation. Clearly, the beneficial effects of social interaction on cognitive growth unfold through the process of on task verbal interaction in discussion (Ben-Ari and Kedem-Fredrich, 2000). As learners become more knowledgeable and experienced with the task, the support is withdrawn, and the children internalise the new knowledge and experiences they have acquired, which results in learning.

From a socio-cultural perspective, both the process (the ways the instruction is delivered and the social interactions that contextualise the learning experience) and the content (the focus of instruction) are of major importance in the understanding of the reading text.

The next to be discussed will be Pearson and Raphael (1990) model of comprehension.

Pearson and Raphael (1990) model of reading comprehension

This model suggests that reading comprehension of text is a complex interactive, dynamic process. This framework recognises that comprehension of text is the product of a complex combination of interactive factors; and these factors influence learners reading comprehension.

Factors that influence learners Reading Comprehension Pearson and Raphael (1990) have identified six interactive layers of factors or variables that they claim influence learners' reading comprehension namely (a) historical/cultural context, (b) the social context, (c) the instructional context, (d) the task environment, (e) the text, and (f) the reader.

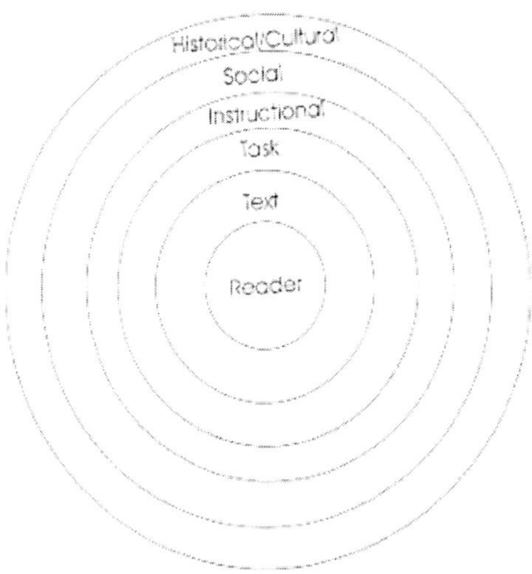

Pearson and Raphael (1990) of reading comprehension.

This model suggest that the six interactive layers of factors namely, (a) historical/cultural context, (b) the social context, (c) the instructional context, (d) the task environment, (e) the text and (f) the reader influence learners reading comprehension. This model is underpinned by interactive view of reading comprehension. Its starting point is developed from the personal experiences of the learner.

Each of the factors will be briefly explained.

Historical/Cultural Context

The reader's cultural beliefs and values influence the comprehension of the text and by belonging to a linguistic group, or an ethnic group, or having a religious or political affiliation, influence the way the reader views the world, thinks, and so comprehends the text (Pearson and Raphael, 1990; Kendeou & van den Broek, 2005). This model suggests that readers comprehend material only if they already know something about the topic. In a way, the readers processing of information may be limited or enhanced by the knowledge base that one processes.

Pang *et al.,* (2003) and Culler, (1975) pointed out that the meanings generated by the learners, depend on how well the learners interpret the language conventions that are used by the author. It is, thus important for reading material for the young learners' needs to be culturally-based so that they are reading from the point of reference. Because texts are written with specific audience in mind, cultural knowledge is present in texts and it is assumed that the reader is familiar with such knowledge (Pang *et al.,* 2003:7).

Social Context

Learning could be perceived as a dynamic process in which the learners play an active role, constantly interacting with the environment and people around them. In social learning model, dialogical interactions between the child and others facilitates the learner's understanding of the vocabulary, the content, and the structural features of the text. In this process learners begin to take responsibility of their own reading and comprehension. Bos and Vaughn (2002) stated that interaction and interdependence were important aspects of the learning environment. In their view, learning could be perceived as a dynamic process in which the learners play an active role, continuously interacting with the environment and people around them. In this way, the environment of the learner becomes important in reading comprehension.

Cambourne (2002) believe that learners should be provided with a rich social literacy environment with a wide variety of genres, and text based interactions with others, effective literacy learning is fostered. In a social leaning model, dialogical interactions between the child and others will automatically facilitates the learner's understanding of the vocabulary, the content and the structural features of the text. During the dialogical process, the learner, learn to take greater responsibility for their own reading strategy use and independence in reading and so comprehension is encouraged (Morgan and Goldstein, 2004). The teachers' responsibility is to give learners constructive feedback for example if the feedback informs and supports the learner on how to resolve text difficulties (Block, 2004). This reading process feedback also encourages learners self evaluate and build on learner's positive self confidence and commitment to task (Hattie, 1992; Volmeyer & Rheinberg, 2005).

Instructional Context

In their research, the RAND Reading Study group (2002:11) explained that learners learning of reading as "the process of simultaneously extracting and constructing meaning through interaction and involvement with written language. This means that learners must be actively involved in their own learning process. It is therefore critical that teachers should have a knowledge base of the various reading comprehension strategies in order to model them appropriately. Researchers have reported that high quality teaching is most important in learner's literacy learning (Westwood, 2004, Pardo, 2004, Pressley, 2002).

Pearson and Raphael (1990) refer to the importance of prior knowledge. They pointed out that learners are aided in the comprehension of what they are reading if there is a prior goal or reason for the reading task. In setting the goals the effective aspects of the reader needs to be taken into consideration, such as motivation to reading, reading attitude and reading interests.

It has to be noted that success in teaching will depend on the knowledge and ability of teachers to find strategies that provide good teaching environment for reading comprehension.

This means that the use of explicit instruction can maximise comprehension. However, learners need to be provided with information on the correct use of the strategy before, during and after reading the text. During this process, corrective feedback regarding the success in effective strategy is vital to help learners to better understand the when, and why of using the strategy. Masttropieri, Scruggs and Goetx (2003), maintained that the more learners understand the use of the strategy and take ownership, the more likely they are to retain and automatically employ that strategy in the future. In a way, strategies should be used interchangeably by the learners in response to the different situation before, during and after reading the text.

The Task Context

It has suggested that the purpose of the reading task and the nature of the text will determine how the reader will approach the comprehension process, and determine which strategies the learner may use when reading. Alfassi, 2004 and Duffy *et al.,* 1987 contends that if the learning task is presented to the reader in an organised and systemic way, reading development is enhanced.

Similarly, Pearson and Raphael, 1990, Pressely, 2002, Durant and Green, 2002, suggest that if the reading task is inherently related to a meaningful activity for the reader, the reader's comprehension of the text is improved (Pearson and Raphael, 1990; Pressely, 2002).

This means that the purpose of the reading task, the nature of the text will determine how the reader will approach the comprehension process; and also determine which strategies the reader may employ when reading. Therefore, the teaching of reading strategies before, during and after reading the text is most critical to help learners in understanding the written text.

The Text Context

Text relevance for the learner is important for the learners to understand the text; and can also be influenced by socio-cultural variables (Freebody and Frieberg, 2001), by the purpose in selecting the text (Burg, 1991) and by how well it is written and organised (Keen, 2002).

Pearson and Raphael (1990) suggested that readers who have a clear understanding of narrative story schema and other types of genre are more successful in the comprehension of that text. This means that within the narrative story context there may also be several sub-plots or incidences that form elements of the larger whole and may assist the learner to understand the story.

What is important about the text context is that for the reader, effective text comprehension results from a combination of cognitive processes that work almost simultaneously and automatically at the word and discourse levels of the text (Baddeley, 1990).

According to Duffy *et al.,* (1986) it is the perception of the text difficulty that stimulates the need to reread, question, infer, or summarise.

The Reader Context

From the graphic representation above, it is clear that the reader of the text is the most important and central element in the Pearson and Raphael (1990) model. All the other elements circles of the model influence the formation of the reader's combination. With respect to the reader, there has been little emphasis upon teaching of reading comprehension in the primary grades. It is important that teachers should have a clear understanding and put more emphasis on the various comprehension strategies.

It is therefore important that before the reading comprehension activity, teachers should know and model effective comprehension strategies to the learners before, during and after reading; to help learners to arrive at a deeper understanding of what they read.

Researchers Lehr and Osborn (2005:17) confirmed that for learners in Grade 3 and up, instruction in specific cognitive strategies can improve reading comprehension for all learners including poor readers. Therefore, what remains a challenge for teachers are what strategies to teach before, during and after reading and how to teach them (Armbruster, Lehr and Osborn, 2001).

Teaching Reading Strategies

When dealing with a reading lesson, students often experience the lack of reading strategies which are essential for them to overcome the challenges in the classroom. Research into reading has found that effective readers are aware of the strategies they use and that they use strategies flexibly and efficiently (Garner, 1987; Presley, Beard EL, Dinary and Brown, 1992). Researchers believed that these strategies could be taught to ineffective language learners so that they can become more successful in language learning. As Oxford (1990:1) states, language learning strategies "...are especially important for language learning because they are tools for active, self-directed movement, which is essential for developing communicative competence. "Therefore, teachers should consider teaching students effective reading strategies, especially showing them how to utilise the skills and knowledge that they bring from their first language in order to cope with reading in the second language.

Besides developing reading proficiency for students, teachers who train students to use reading strategies can also help them become autonomous language learners. As a result, teaching students learning strategies is an important duty of the language teacher since learning strategies can help students monitor and take charge of the own learning. Helping students understand good language learning strategies and training them to develop and use such good language strategies can be considered to be the appreciated characteristics of a good language teacher (Lessard-Clouston, 1997:3).

Reading strategies are important to assist the reader to read the text with understanding, identify relevant and non-relevant information from the text. It is therefore critical that teachers should develop learners' awareness of the reading process and reading strategies and their use. Learners should practice a variety of strategies by using real text and teach them to learn to read to learn. During reading, teachers must demonstrate the strategies that will work best for the specific type of text and context. Teachers must encourage learners to practice the learnt strategies outside the class in their reading tasks. Pressley (1998) agrees, and suggests that to become competent readers, children need to learn two things: word identification strategies and comprehension strategies. These strategies are interdependent, with comprehension being closely linked with a reader's swift and efficient identification of the words in a text.

Struggling readers often do not employ strategies to aid reading comprehension and need assistance to use strategies (Jetton, Rupley and Willson, 1995).Various authors agree that teaching reading strategies to learners to become more strategic and metacognitive in their approach to reading (Ariel,1992) can enhance their learners comprehension. This means that metacognitive instruction is important in reading. This is because metacognitive proponents' belief that:

That the Students can be Taught

Clay (1991:333-340) divides reading strategies in three categories:

Strategies which maintain fluency. This category helps learners in using their knowledge of oral language and comprehension of words to predict and read fluently.

Strategies which detect and correct error. These are strategies which help learners to use meaning, structure and visual information to confirm reading (self-monitoring) and notice mistakes and correct them based on new information (self-correction).

Strategies for problem-solving new words. These are strategies for problem-solving new words. They can assist learners to check one information cue with another information cue to understand new words (cross-checking).

Comprehension strategies are very important in reading. They reflect a purposeful, intentional, on-going, and adaptable plan, procedure, or process to improve reading performance; because without it, learners have virtually no means to increase the sophistication of their reading (Philips, Norris and Vavra, 2007). According to Shanahan (2006: 28), comprehension strategies are intentional actions that a reader can take to increase their chances of understanding or remembering the information in a text. Comprehension strategies are important in that they provide the reader with knowledge of how to use the strategies appropriately and understand the text (NRP, 2000; Pressley *et al.,* 1998; Shanahan *et al.,* 2010). This implies that teaching reading comprehension is basic for comprehension.

As far as practical application is concerned there are cognitive and metacognitive strategies.

The development of metacognition skills is important in learners. Metacognition strategies are critical to stimulate thinking. This varies from learners to learners. If acquired appropriately, metacognition strategies may assist learners to self-regulate their own learning. According to Flavell (1976:232), metacognition means awareness of one's thought processes in the act of carrying them out. The human being then uses this awareness to control him/herself. Metacognition makes the person aware of the way in which he/she is thinking. Good readers use metacognition strategies to think about and have control over their reading. For example, before reading, they might clarify their purpose for reading and preview the text. During reading, they might monitor their understanding, adjusting their reading speed to fit the difficulty of the text and fixing up any comprehension problems they have. After reading, they check their understanding of what they read (Beck, McKeown, Hamilton and Kucan, 2003).

Metacognitive strategies are higher-order executive tactics that entail planning for learning, monitoring, identifying and remedying causes of comprehension failure or evaluating the successes of a learning activity, that is, the strategies of self-planning, self-monitoring, self-regulating, self-questioning and self-reflecting (Pressley and Afflerbach, 1995; O'Malley and Chamot, 1990; Zimmerman, 1998). Metacognitive strategies involve planning, monitoring and evaluating before, during and after any thinking act such as reading comprehension. Cognitive strategies involve direct interaction with the text and contribute to facilitating comprehension, and operate directly on incoming information, manipulating it in ways that enhance learning (Anastasiou and Griva, 2009:284). Cognitive strategies include the strategies of underlining, using titles, using dictionary, writing down, guessing from the context, imagery, activating prior knowledge, summarising, using linguistic clues, using text markers, skipping the difficult parts and repeating phrases (Anastasiou and Griva, 2009:284). Good readers employ different cognitive and metacognitive strategies before, during and after reading a text. Given the complexity of comprehension, it seems likely that learners may fail to understand what they have read for a variety of reasons; hence, teaching reading is critical. Therefore, comprehension strategies are needed if one is to accomplish the task of teaching reading comprehension.

To understand written text, learners need to decode printed words and access their meanings. The question is whether teachers are doing enough to help learners to read, evaluate information and use it in their daily lives, and when the teaching of reading comprehension should begin. Should it begin when children are still very young, when they are older or even in the adolescent years? I believe that we must start in the early childhood years; in fact, teaching reading comprehension should be the goal of the primary grades. I believe that by the time learners are in Grade 3, they should be able to read the text and grasp its meaning, and be able to use the information in other situations in their lives. Zimmerman (1998) is of the opinion that learners at all levels are significantly influenced by the type of opportunities they are given. If they are given tasks that make them think, and thinking is mediated, they will do so; but if they are not given tasks in which they can practice any comprehension strategies then they will not do so. I believe that the earlier we start teaching learners comprehension strategies, the better.

The alternative–not teaching comprehension strategies–would be to believe that comprehension and thought processes are a function area of heredity and are fixed when the child is born. Cognition is a function of both heredity and environment, and environmental factors can be manipulated to influence comprehension. In this regard, if comprehension strategies are really patterns of behaviour, then we might expect that practice would still have a positive effect on learners. Practice will lead to competence in intellectual functions, some of which will take place automatically in appropriate contexts. This does not mean that there is nothing more that affects the development of reading comprehension, but it means that practising strategies is the most important aspect.

Piaget (1950; 1953) stated that children adapt themselves to their environment through assimilation and accommodation. As they do this they learn to think and comprehend because they are striving to maintain a state of equilibrium between themselves and the environment. Although Piaget was not really trying to prove that comprehension can be taught, his theory seems to support it, because it implies that cognition can develop by interacting with the environment. This leads me to the assumption that if the environment is manipulated with the aim of improving the learner's thinking, then comprehension can be taught and learnt; and then comprehension strategies can be taught.

Relating to Piaget's theory, teaching reading comprehension evolves through stages, meaning that there may be certain comprehension strategies that can be taught and some that cannot, due to the maturational levels of these learners. However, cognitive psychologists have found that young children can perform cognitive tasks that were originally regarded as being too advanced for them and, therefore can be taught comprehension strategies that were supposedly too advanced for them. For example, it has been found that children can understand cause and effect more than Piaget had given them credit for. Different authors on the subject concur that reading can be taught as they are given suitable tasks and appropriate information and mediation.

Reading Comprehension Strategies

Comprehension strategies are important in the lives of learners. Philips, Norris and Vavra (2007) and Kirby (2007) confirm that without them, learners have virtually no means of increasing the sophistication of reading. Teachers need to employ research-based strategies in the classroom because they have scientific evidence of success stories. Comprehension is not just something that just happens it needs to be taught. According to Shanahan (2006:31), drilling and repetition will not help in the teaching of reading comprehension; however, sound explanation of comprehension strategies and their importance is central. They believe that training of teachers in how to teach reading comprehension remains an important aspect. Teachers need knowledge and skills to monitor learners' comprehension and teach learners comprehension strategies. That means before reading, the teacher carries the responsibility by providing a demonstration. According to Shanahan (2006:31), the demonstration must include a clear explanation of the strategy, a description of how and when to use it, and lastly an explanation of why it is useful. This relates to the theory of Vygotsky (1987), that for the child to develop to a stage where they can learn, they have to be in the company of a role model. The most important people in the context of this study are the teachers. If they do not serve as positive role models, the learner will never develop and become able to read and understand the text. During shared reading, group guided reading, independent reading and reading aloud, the teacher must use various strategies for example summarising, story structure to teach reading comprehension.

From the discussions above, there seems to be a wealth of research evidence showing that reading comprehension can be improved by teaching learners comprehension strategies. According to Lenz (2005:2) and Armbruster *et al.,* (2003:45-57) it would be appropriate and easier for teachers to follow the three ways of organising comprehension strategies and to think about strategies that one might use, before reading (phase 1), during reading (phase 2) and after reading (phase 3). This is because reading comprehension is a process, and as such it has various stages at which different tasks need to be performed. The purpose of the before-reading strategies is to activate prior knowledge for text comprehension. Before reading, learners learn new information by connecting it to what they already know about a topic and the structure of a text (Pressley *et al.,* 1998). During reading comprehension, learners read books and stories from the past, and use language to write their own bibliography. Learners should be able to read with understanding, and where difficulties occur, be able to initiate repair strategies if comprehension breakdown is detected. During reading comprehension, learners read non-fiction stories, big books with various topics in nature, explaining simple facts, simple weather forecasts, stories about the sun and moon, for example. Learners activate prior knowledge, make connections among important ideas, construct and test hypotheses, paraphrase key points, and try to resolve any comprehension difficulties that may arise (Pressley *et al.,* 1997). After-reading helps learners to clarify any unclear meaning and where learners maybe required answering questions in writing–either comprehension questions at the end of a chapter or questions handed out by the teacher.

Reading comprehension is a cognitive process that involves a deliberate, strategic problem-solving action of the reader as he or she engages with a text. In this process readers use their prior knowledge, reading comprehension strategies, knowledge of language and print, experience and perceived purpose of reading. From the theoretical point of view, if the knowledgeable teacher actively involves learners, the teaching of reading comprehension can increase the chances of understanding or remembering the information in a text. The teacher's knowledge of teaching comprehension strategies and willingness, and the classroom learning environment may influence the way the learner views the text. It implies that the teacher should be able to teach strategies as a way to help the learners to comprehend the text. Learners come from home into contact with the teacher who is required to teach learners how to construct meaning from the text by using the strategies for before, during and after reading. My argument is that the teachers' use of reading comprehension strategies may influence reading comprehension positively.

According to Noles and Dole (2004:179), the teaching of strategies empowers readers, particularly those who struggle, by giving them the tools they need to construct meaning from text. They further explain that instead of blaming comprehension problems on learners' own innate abilities for which they (learners) see no solution, explicit strategy instruction teaches learners to take control of their own learning and comprehension. Loranger (1997:31) found that learners who were trained in the use of strategies showed greater focus of engagement during reading groups, improved knowledge use of strategies, and improved achievement in comprehension (Zimmerman,1998).

In the same vein, Dreyer (1998:23) in her study used the reading comprehension strategies to train learners in reading comprehension; and the results showed that instruction in reading comprehension strategies can and do make a very important contribution in improving the reading comprehension of learners. These research studies demonstrate that reading comprehension strategies can be taught and that they can contribute to improve learners' reading comprehension abilities.

The NRP (2000) examined research studies that focused on learners in K-12 (Grades R-12) and concluded that there was sufficient evidence supporting the teaching of seven comprehension strategies. These strategies are comprehension monitoring, graphic and semantic organisers, question answering, question generating, story structure, summarising and multiple strategies. There is a need for the teachers to teach comprehension strategies to help learners to read with understanding. Strategies, if used appropriately in classrooms, may help teachers to teach the learners how to unlock the code of written text with ease. In the following section, I present the primary reading comprehension strategies based on research evidence as identified by the NRP (2000). If applied correctly, they may be effective in teaching reading comprehension.

Metacognitive Strategies

> One approach in assisting children's reading involves a cycle of modelled reading (teacher reading to children), guided reading (teacher reading with children) and independent reading (children reading on their own) (Luke, 1993).
>
> The second theory related to the intervention is metacognition. Metacognition involves directing one's own reading, making decisions about how to approach particular passages.

The term metacognition was introduced by Flavell in 1979 to refer to 'the individual's own awareness and consideration of his or her cognitive processes and strategies'. It refers to individual capability to think about their own thinking. Metacognition involves processes such as self-questioning, prediction and monitoring the information in a text while reading (Nolan, 1991). There is empirical evidence (NRP, 2000; Singhal, 2001; Mayer, 2003; Trabassco and Bouchard, 2002; Philips, Norris and Vavra, 2007) in the literature that the use of metacognitive strategies leads to better reading comprehension performance in learners. Research study in the area of reading comprehension by Mokharti and Reichard (2002), Pressley (2002), Anderson (2000), Taberski (2000) and NICHD (2000) has led to an increasing emphasis on the role of metacognitive awareness, which has been defined as the perceived use of reading strategies while reading. Metacognitive strategies are higher-order executive tactics that entail planning for learning, monitoring, identifying and remediating causes of comprehension failure or evaluating the successes of a learning activity; that is, the strategies of self-planning, self-monitoring, self-regulating, self-questioning and self-reflecting (Pressley and Afflerbach, 1995; O'Malley and Chamot, 1990; Zimmerman, 1998). O'Malley and Chamot (1990) emphasise that the lack of metacognitive approaches in learners results in a lack of direction and an inability to self-monitor their progress, accomplishments and future learning directions. Research in the area of reading comprehension has led to an increasing emphasis on the role of metacognitive awareness, which has been defined as the perceived use of reading strategies while reading (Mokharti and Reichard, 2002; Pressley, 2002).

Metacognition can be defined as 'thinking about thinking' (Philips, Norris and Vavra, 2007:4) and metacognitive strategies activate one's thinking and lead to improved performance in learning (Anderson, 1991, 2002). Good readers use metacognition strategies to think about their own reading and have control over this process. For example, before reading, learners might clarify their reason for reading and previewing the text (Pressley, 2002). During reading, they might monitor their understanding, adjusting their reading speed to fit the difficulty of the text and fixing up any comprehension problems they have. After reading, they check their understanding of what they read.

Metacognition Approach

Reading strategies provide "an overall plan to gain meaning from text. Often termed 'metacognition,' these strategies include scanning the text, sampling, predicting, confirming, understanding and correcting errors as they occur" (Winch *et al.,* 2001, p. 44). Strategies develop with age and experience, are important for effective reading and must be taught. Research indicates that comprehension monitoring is a developmental skill that is not fully mastered until adolescence. For example, Brown and Day (1983) and Brown, Day and Jones (1983) found that low-ability students did not always benefit from instruction in monitoring strategies. These strategies may be beneficial only if students have the background and understanding to use them effectively. However, with attention to students' level of maturity, aspects of comprehension monitoring can be taught. It is important that teachers model actually using these strategies rather than teaching about the strategies (Meir, 1984). There is empirical evidence (NRP, 2000; Singhal, 2001; Mayer, 2003; Trabassco and Bouchard, 2002; Philips, Norris and Vavra, 2007) in the literature that the use of metacognitive strategies leads to better reading comprehension performance in learners. Research study in the area of reading comprehension by Mokhartiand Reichard (2002), Pressley (2002), Anderson (2000), Taberski (2000) and NICHD (2000) has led to an increasing emphasis on the role of metacognitive awareness, which has been defined as the perceived use of reading strategies while reading. Metacognitive strategies are higher-order executive tactics that entail planning for learning, monitoring, identifying and remediating causes of comprehension failure or evaluating the successes of a learning activity; that is, the strategies of self-planning, self-monitoring, self-regulating, self-questioning and self-reflecting (Pressley and Afflerbach, 1995; O'Malley and Chamot, 1990; Zimmerman, 1998). O'Malley and Chamot (1990) emphasise that the lack of metacognitive approaches in learners results in a lack of direction and an inability to self-monitor their progress, accomplishments and future learning directions. Research in the area of reading comprehension has led to an increasing emphasis on the role of metacognitive awareness, which has been defined as the perceived use of reading strategies while reading (Mokharti and Reichard, 2002; Pressley, 2002).

As mentioned earlier, Rhoder (2002) describes a model of strategy instruction designed to promote mindful reading so that students understand, select and monitor strategies as they read. This model involves instruction within the students ZPD (the area of skill they are capable of learning with the help of an expert), explicit modelling, practice and opportunities to transfer their use of metacognition strategies into new situations.

To help students develop metecognitive strategies, teachers must encourage them to become active learners. For example, students need to set goals for their reading tasks, to plan how they will meet their goals, to monitor their success in meeting their goals, and to remedy the situation when they do not meet their goals. This involves knowing certain techniques, such as relating new information to their background knowledge, previewing material to be read, paraphrasing ideas presented, and identifying the organisational pattern of text. Students need to learn the value of periodically questioning themselves about their ideas in a text to see if they are meeting goals (Babbs and Moe, 1983).

Metacognitive skills associated with meta language awareness programme

Current research identifies characteristics which differentiate skilled readers from unskilled readers. For example, unskilled readers focus on decoding single words, and fail to adjust their reading for different texts and purposes (Paris, Wasik and Turner, 1990). Similarly, poor readers tend to be non-strategic and are unable to ameliorate comprehension failure (Mercer, 1992). Skilled readers on the other hand are engaged in active learning strategies. They use good monitoring strategies whereby they establish goals for an instructional activity, determine the degree to which they are being met, and, if necessary, change the strategies being used to attain the goal (Rubin, 1997). The suggestion is that skilled readers know what to do, as well as how and when to do it, they have the metacognitive abilities that make them active consumers of information.

Three clusters of metacognitive skills are identified in the literature (Foreman, 2001).

These Include:

- Being aware of a level of understanding by identifying inconsistency and inaccuracies while reading;
- Monitoring that the goals for reading are being achieved and that effective strategies are being used to achieve these goals;
- Regulating the use of strategies to ensure that they assist faltering comprehension (for example, re-reading, self-questioning) (p. 204).

The underlying assumption behind metacognitive instruction is that students with learning difficulties are characteristically non-strategic in their approach to learning and are generally lacking in metacognitive ability (Mercer, 1992). More importantly however, metacognitive approaches maintain that through appropriate instruction a learner can become "an active rather than passive participant in one's own thinking" (Kulieke and Fly-Jones, 1993). In other words, the poor reader can learn to become metacognitive. Indeed, it is acknowledged that students with learning difficulties need more direct teaching in the form of metacognitive training, especially if they are going to achieve results comparable to those of their average peers (Turner, 1992).

Metacognitive Instruction

As stated earlier, research in reading has identified several characteristics that differentiate skilled readers from unskilled readers. For example, unskilled readers "focus on decoding single words, fail to adjust their reading for different texts and purposes and seldom look ahead or look ahead or back to monitor and improve their comprehension" (Paris *et al.,* 1990, p. 609). Similarly, poor readers tend to be non-strategic. For example, poor readers focus energy on looking busy and following directions, but remain unaware of comprehension difficulties or strategies for ameliorating comprehension failure (Duffy and Roehler, 1989; Paris *et al.,* 1990). Many unskilled readers believe that the purpose of reading is to pronounce words correctly. When asked to summarise a passage, they often recite sentences from the text verbatim without conveying an understanding of the material (Baker and Brown, 1984; Paris and Jacobs, 1984).

The Aim of Metacognitive Instruction

Develop the sensitivity of students to learning situations, to heighten students' awareness of their own cognitive repertoire and the factors that affect the learning process and contribute to successful learning, to teach strategies for learning, and to develop students' capacity to regulate and monitor their activities (Ariel, 1992, p. 82).

Therefore, the aim is to have students become self-regulated learners, learners who can monitor, evaluate and control their own learning (Harris and Pressley, 1991).

Research studies have demonstrated that poor readers do not routinely engage in contructive activities required for good comprehension during reading. These activities include clarifying the purpose of reading, focusing attention on important parts of the text, constantly checking for understanding and taking appropriate actions when breakdowns in comprehension occur, asking oneself questions during reading to enhance recall and making predictions (Chan, 1991). Metacognitive models of instruction emphasise that successful readers are "good strategy users" (Duffy and Roehler, 1989). In particular, metacognitive model endeavour to teach students how to adapt and apply strategies to multiple setting, that is to generalise their use of strategies across time and setting (Hay, 1995).

Students must learn to adopt task-appropriate goals; to generate, select and/or adapt strategies appropriately based on tasks and relevant content knowledge; and to monitor progress and adjust approaches as necessary. They must also construct knowledge (about tasks, strategies and specific domains) and beliefs (perceptions of self-efficacy and attributions) that support self-regulation (Butler, 1995, p.171).

Comprehension Strategies

Comprehension strategies are important in the lives of learners. Philips, Norris and Vavra (2007) and Kirby (2007) confirm that without them, learners have virtually no means of increasing the sophistication of reading. Teachers need to employ research-based strategies in the classroom because they have scientific evidence of success stories. Comprehension is not just something that just happens it needs to be taught. According to Shanahan (2006:31), drilling and repetition will not help in the teaching of reading comprehension; however, sound explanation of comprehension strategies and their importance is central. They believe that training of teachers in how to teach reading comprehension remains an important aspect. Teachers need knowledge and skills to monitor learners' comprehension and teach learners comprehension strategies. That means before reading, the teacher carries the responsibility by providing a demonstration. According to Shanahan (2006:31), the demonstration must include a clear explanation of the strategy, a description of how and when to use it, and lastly an explanation of why it is useful. This relates to the theory of Vygotsky (1987), that for the child to develop to a stage where they can learn, they have to be in the company of a role model. If teachers do not serve as positive role models, the learner will never develop and become able to read and understand the text. During shared reading, group guided reading, independent reading and reading aloud, the teacher must use various strategies for example summarising, story structure to teach reading comprehension.

There seems to be a wealth of research evidence showing that reading comprehension can be improved by teaching learners comprehension strategies. According to Lenz (2005:2) and Armbruster *et al.,* (2003:45-57) it would be appropriate and easier for teachers to follow the three ways of organising comprehension strategies and to think about strategies that one might use, before reading (phase 1), during reading (phase 2) and after reading (phase 3). This is because reading comprehension is a process, and as such it has various stages at which different tasks need to be performed. The purpose of the before-reading strategies is to activate prior knowledge for text comprehension. Before reading, learners learn new information by connecting it to what they already know about a topic and the structure of a text (Pressley *et al.,* 1998). During reading comprehension, learners read books and stories from the past, and use language to write their own bibliography. Learners should be able to read with understanding, and where difficulties occur, be able to initiate repair strategies if comprehension breakdown is detected. During reading comprehension, learners read non-fiction stories, big books with various topics in nature, explaining simple facts, simple weather forecasts, stories about the sun and moon, for example. Learners activate prior knowledge, make connections among important ideas, construct and test hypotheses, paraphrase key points, and try to resolve any comprehension difficulties that may arise (Pressley *et al.,* 1997). After-reading helps learners to clarify any unclear meaning and where learners maybe required answering questions in writing–either comprehension questions at the end of a chapter or questions handed out by the teacher.

Reading comprehension is a cognitive process that involves a deliberate, strategic problem-solving action of the reader as he or she engages with a text. In this process readers use their prior knowledge, reading comprehension strategies, knowledge of language and print, experience and perceived purpose of reading. From the theoretical point of view, if the knowledgeable teacher actively involves learners, the teaching of reading comprehension can increase the chances of understanding or remembering the information in a text. The teacher's knowledge of teaching comprehension strategies and willingness, and the classroom learning environment may influence the way the learner views the text. In the context of the study, it implies that the teacher should be able to teach strategies as a way to help the learners to comprehend the text. Learners come from home into contact with the teacher who is required to teach learners how to construct meaning from the text by using the strategies for before, during and after reading. My argument is that the teachers' use of reading comprehension strategies may influence reading comprehension positively.

According to Noles and Dole (2004:179), the teaching of strategies empowers readers, particularly those who struggle, by giving them the tools they need to construct meaning from text. They further explain that instead of blaming comprehension problems on learners' own innate abilities for which they (learners) see no solution, explicit strategy instruction teaches learners to take control of their own learning and comprehension. Loranger (1997:31) found that learners who were trained in the use of strategies showed greater focus of engagement during reading groups, improved knowledge use of strategies, and improved achievement in comprehension (Zimmerman,1998).

In the same vein, Dreyer (1998:23) in her study used the reading comprehension strategies to train learners in reading comprehension; and the results showed that instruction in reading comprehension strategies can and do make a very important contribution in improving the reading comprehension of learners. These research studies demonstrate that reading comprehension strategies can be taught and that they can contribute to improve learners' reading comprehension abilities.

The NRP (2000) examined research studies that focused on learners in K-12 (Grades R-12) and concluded that there was sufficient evidence supporting the teaching of seven comprehension strategies. These strategies are comprehension monitoring, graphic and semantic organisers, question answering, question generating, story structure, summarising and multiple strategies.

Comprehension strategies are important in the lives of learners. Philips, Norris and Vavra (2007) and Kirby (2007) confirm that without them, learners have virtually no means of increasing the sophistication of reading. Teachers need to employ research-based strategies in the classroom because they have scientific evidence of success stories. Comprehension is not just something that just happens it needs to be taught. According to Shanahan (2006:31), drilling and repetition will not help in the teaching of reading comprehension. However, sound explanation of comprehension strategies and their importance is central.

It is thus believed that training teachers in how to teach reading comprehension remains an important aspect. Teachers need knowledge and skills to monitor learners' comprehension and teach learners comprehension strategies. That means before reading, the teacher carries the responsibility by providing a demonstration. According to Shanahan (2006:31), the demonstration must include a clear explanation of the strategy, a description of how and when to use it, and lastly an explanation of why it is useful. This relates to the theory of Vygotsky (1987), that for the child to develop to a stage where they can learn, they have to be in the company of a role model. The most important people in the context of this study are the teachers. If they do not serve as positive role models, the learner will never develop and become able to read and understand the text. During shared reading, group guided reading, independent reading and reading aloud, the teacher must use various strategies for example summarising, story structure to teach reading comprehension.

From the discussions above, there seems to be a wealth of research evidence showing that reading comprehension can be improved by teaching learners comprehension strategies. According to Lenz (2005:2) and Armbruster *et al.,* (2003:45-57), it would be appropriate and easier for teachers to follow the three ways of organising comprehension strategies and to think about strategies that one might use, before reading (phase 1), during reading (phase 2) and after reading (phase 3). This is because reading comprehension is a process, and as such, it has various stages at which different tasks need to be performed.

The purpose of the before-reading strategies is to activate prior knowledge for text comprehension. Before reading, learners learn new information by connecting it to what they already know about a topic and the structure of a text (Pressley *et al.,* 1998).

During reading comprehension, learners read books and stories from the past, and use language to write their own bibliography. Learners should be able to read with understanding, and where difficulties occur, be able to initiate repair strategies if comprehension breakdown is detected. During reading comprehension, learners read non-fiction stories, big books with various topics in, for example, nature, explaining simple facts, simple weather forecasts, and stories about the sun and moon. Learners activate prior knowledge, make connections among important ideas, construct and test hypotheses, paraphrase key points, and try to resolve any comprehension difficulties that may arise (Pressley *et al.,* 1997).

After-reading helps learners to clarify any unclear meaning and where learners maybe required answering questions in writing – either comprehension questions at the end of a chapter or questions handed out by the teacher.

Reading comprehension is a cognitive process that involves a deliberate, strategic problem-solving action of the reader as he or she engages with a text. In this process, readers use their prior knowledge, reading comprehension strategies, knowledge of language and print, experience and perceived purpose of reading. From the theoretical point of view, if the knowledgeable teacher actively involves learners, the teaching of reading comprehension can increase the chances of understanding or remembering the information in a text. The teacher's knowledge of teaching comprehension strategies and willingness, and the classroom learning environment may influence the way the learner views the text. In the context of the study, it implies that the teacher should be able to teach strategies as a way to help the learners to comprehend the text. Learners come from home into contact with the teacher who is required to teach learners how to construct meaning from the text by using the strategies for before, during and after reading. My argument is that the teachers' use of reading comprehension strategies may influence reading comprehension positively.

According to Noles and Dole (2004:179), the teaching of strategies empowers readers, particularly those who struggle, by giving them the tools they need to construct meaning from text. They further explain that instead of blaming comprehension problems on learners' own innate abilities for which they (learners) see no solution, explicit strategy instruction teaches learners to take control of their own learning and comprehension. Loranger (1997:31) found that learners who were trained in the use of strategies showed greater focus of engagement during reading groups, improved knowledge use of strategies, and improved achievement in comprehension (Zimmerman,1998).

In the same vein, Dreyer (1998:23) used the reading comprehension strategies to train learners in reading comprehension in her study, and the results showed that instruction in reading comprehension strategies can and do make a very important contribution in improving the reading comprehension of learners. These research studies demonstrate that reading comprehension strategies can be taught and that they can contribute to improve learners' reading comprehension abilities.

In America, because of the low level of reading comprehension amongst the learners, the NRP (2000) examined research studies that focused on learners in K-12 (Grades R-12) and concluded that there was sufficient evidence supporting the teaching of seven comprehension strategies. These strategies are comprehension monitoring, graphic and semantic organisers, question answering, question generating, story structure, summarising and multiple strategies.

Within the context of my research project based on the low performance of Grade 3 learners, in particular Tshivenda-speaking learners, there is a need for the teachers to teach comprehension strategies to help learners to read with understanding. My argument is that these strategies, if used in a Tshivenda classroom, may help teachers to teach the learners how to unlock the code of written text with ease. In the following section, I present the primary reading comprehension strategies based on research evidence as identified by the NRP (2000). These comprehension strategies are relevant as they can be used within the context of my study. If applied correctly, they may be effective in teaching reading comprehension to Tshivenda-speaking learners.

Comprehension Monitoring

The teaching and monitoring of comprehension strategies are important to assist the reader to become aware of and realised that when they read they understand what they are reading. This refers to learners' knowledge about and use of reading comprehension strategies, and is a form of metacognition. Routman (2000:134) defines comprehension monitoring as "a metacognitive process which is affected by person strategy and task variables." Routman (2000:134) adds to this by stating that comprehensive monitoring is essential for reading as it directs the reader when trying to make sense of a text. Good readers use metacognitive strategies to think about and have control over their reading, for example, before reading, they might monitor their understanding, adjusting their reading speed to fit the difficulty of the text and 'fix-up' any comprehension problems they have. After reading, they check their understanding of what they read. Examples of fix-up strategies are identifying where in the text the difficulty occurs, restarting a difficult sentence or passage on their own and looking back (or forward) through the text (Lehr and Osborn, 2005:18).

According to Lehr and Osborn (2000:18), readers learn how to be aware of understanding their material during comprehension monitoring (NRP, 2000:15). Lehr and Osborn (2003) regard the reader's thinking as important during the comprehension processes. Specifically, it teaches learners to notice when they understand, to identify what they do not understand, and to use appropriate fix-up strategies to resolve the problems when they do not understand something they read (NRP, 2000; Armbruster *et al.*, 2003; Lehr & Osborn, 2005). This implies that when learners monitor their comprehension, they understand that reading must make sense; and when it does not they try to use appropriate different fix-up strategies to resolve the problems. The goal is to develop awareness by readers of the cognitive process involved during reading and teaches learners to be aware of what they do understand. The NRP (2000) suggested that monitoring comprehension strategies could help learners to become more aware of their difficulties during reading comprehension.

In teaching comprehension monitoring strategies, the teacher needs to demonstrate awareness of difficulties of understanding words, phrases, clauses or sentences. Learners are taught to think about what is hampering their understanding. They think aloud, reread, slow down, and look back in text to try to solve a problem (Armbruster *et al.*, 2003:6-7).

Context clues are also an important part of comprehension monitoring. Learners can use this strategy during reading when they encounter an unfamiliar word in text, for example, when a learner stumbles on an unfamiliar word, she/he needs to know how to use all word identification tools in their mental toolbox to decode the word. Learners look to see if they recognise any part of the word and then say the beginning sound of the familiar part of the word, and then read the rest of the sentence. If learners cannot say the correct word, then the teacher asks them to think what would make sense there, reminding the learners to use all clues.

Graphic and Semantic Organisers

Another comprehension strategy that is important to reading comprehension is the used of graphic and semantic organisers. These tools enable learners to examine and visually represent relationships and help learners write well-organised summaries. These organisers illustrate concepts and interrelationships among concepts of text, using diagrams or other pictorial devices (Armbruster *et al.*, 2003:50). Graphic and semantic organisers are found in many forms, for example, semantic maps, expository maps, story maps and graphic metaphors. These allow the reader to represent graphically/visually the meanings and relationships of concepts and their relationships with other concepts (Armbruster *et al.,* 2003; Lehr and Osborn, 2005). Lehr and Osborn (2005:19) expand the description by saying that graphic and semantic organisers allow the reader to represent graphically/visually the meanings and relationships of the ideas that underlie the words in the text and to improve a reader's memory of what they read. By using the strategy of graphic and semantic organisers, readers focus on concepts and how they are related to other concepts. In teaching the use of graphic and semantic organisers, the teacher must ask learners to construct an image that represents the content.

Questioning

The strategy of asking and answering questions seems to have been used for many years and is still used by teachers to guide and monitor learners' learning. Questions appear to be effective for improving learners' reading comprehension. They provide learners with a purpose for reading, helps learners to focus attention on what they are to learn, help learners to think actively as they read, encourage learners to monitor their comprehension, and help learners to review content and relate what they have learnt to what they already know.

In her study, Durkin (1978) criticise the asking and answering questions as a reading comprehension strategy. She points out that the manner in which teachers ask questions is more of an assessment of comprehension rather than teaching of the reading comprehension process, and regards it as 'interrogation'. However, it is important for teachers to ask various questions to develop learners' critical thinking. Bloom (1986) and Joubert *et al.* (2008) agree that the type of questions learners become accustomed to can shape their understanding of the text, for example, when learners are constantly asked literal questions, they will obviously focus on these during reading comprehension. Routman (1996:137) maintains that teachers need to ask higher-order questions and show learners how to find answers, and this requires interactive settings in order to achieve high levels of reading comprehension. The teacher's questioning strongly supports and advances learners' learning from reading, keeps the learners engaged and enhances understanding (Feldman, 2003).

Analysis by Zimmerman and Hutchins (2003) on questioning as a strategy indicates that "questions lead readers deeper into a piece, setting up dialogue with the author, sparking in readers' minds what they care about. If you ask questions as you read, you are awake, you are interacting with words" (Zimmerman and Hutchins, 2003:73).

This implies that questioning during reading becomes a strategy to help learners to learn to interact with the author of the text and so remain focused throughout the text. Teachers must ask a combination of questions and show learners how to find answers. This can be done by discussing the different types of questions that exist with the learners (Raphael and Au, 2005) and using the information to locate the answer.

In order to succeed, Taylor, Pearson, Peterson and Rodriguez (2002) and Bloom (1968) found that learners must engage in high levels of questioning and do so in highly interactive settings to achieve high levels of comprehension. In a way, it is critical that instruction should help learners understand that active readers question the author, the text, and themselves before, during and after reading.

Raphael and Au (2005) maintain that in order for learners to be able to answer higher-order questions, they need to be able to understand the relationship between the question and the answer. Under questioning as a comprehension strategy, there are two different strategies, namely question answering and question generating.

Question Answering

During reading comprehension, the teacher expects the learner to read and understand the text and answer questions, and to use the information when needed. The teaching of the question-answering strategy is helpful for the learners as they become aware of what is important in the text and learn to answer the questions.

During question answering, the reader answers questions posed by the teacher and is given feedback for correctness. It gives learners a purpose for reading, focuses attention on what they are to learn, encourages them to monitor and helps them to review content and relate what they have learnt to what they already know. Learners learn to distinguish questions that can be answered based on the text from those based on prior knowledge. They are encouraged to learn to answer questions better and therefore acquire more knowledge (Armbruster *et al.,* 2003:49-53). There are different types of questions, for example, answering instructions, which simply teaches learners to re-examine the text to find answers to questions that they could not answer after the initial reading. Another type of questions help learners understand the relationship between questions and where the answers to those questions are found. In this instruction, readers learn to answer questions that require an understanding of information.

Questioning during the guided reading phase is intended to scaffold learning for learners and to check learners' understanding. Such questioning is meant to instruct, guide learners along the pathway to independence (Dewitz, 2006).

When teaching the question answering strategy, teachers need to ask learners questions during and after reading passages of text. Teachers ask learners to look back. Within the context of this study, 'looking back' is when learners articulates and process their understanding of what they have read and to find answers after reading. Teachers ask learners to analyse questions with respect to whether the question is tapping literal information covered in the text, information that can be inferred by combining information in the text, or information in the reader's prior knowledge base (NRP, 2000).

Concerning the type of questions to be asked, Joubert *et al.*, (2008) recommend Bloom's and other taxonomies as useful tools for helping teachers to engage learners in higher-order thinking when they read. We can also relate this higher-order thinking with the applied model of self-regulation of Zimmerman (1998). Teachers must identify each learner's abilities and match their profile to a variety of reading comprehension strategies rather than teach in a rigid manner. If learners apply higher-order thinking, they are able to draw more meaning from what they learn and apply the learning in more sophisticated ways. Although thinking skills alone do not make a learner an effective reader, they are essential for reading comprehension.

Question Generation

Teachers expect learners to become independent and lifelong readers. Readers who attain this learn to ask themselves questions about various aspects of the story (NRP, 2000; Lehr and Osborn, 2005).

Question generating encourages the learner to be actively involved and learn to own the reading text, and thus improves comprehension ability (Routman, 1994:139). In their view, Lehr and Osborn (2005) confirm that teaching learners to ask their own questions improves their active processing of text and improves their comprehension. By generating questions, learners become aware of whether they can answer the questions and if they understand what they are reading. Learners learn to ask themselves questions that require them to integrate information from different segments of text, for example, learners can be taught to ask main idea questions that relate to important information in a text. Question generating teaches learners to become involved in the text, independently. They learn to become active readers and self-questioners and to become aware of whether they understand the text or not. As a result, their overall comprehension improves (Duke and Pearson, 2002).

In teaching the question-generating strategy, teachers need to ask learners to generate questions while reading a passage. The question should integrate information across different parts of the passage. Teachers ask learners to evaluate their questions, checking that they covered important material, were integrative, and whether they could be answered based on what was in the text. Teachers provide feedback on the quality of the questions asked or assist learners in answering the question generated (Armbruster *et al.,* 2003:11).

Question generating also assist learners to increase their awareness of whether they are comprehending text (NRP, 2000; Armbruster *et al.,* 2003). Questioning can be applied before, during and after reading. Pearson (1984:727) suggests that during reading comprehension, teachers should make sure that guided reading questions (asked either during or after stories) include many inference questions to enhance both story-specific inferential comprehension and comprehension of new stories. Secondly, adding a pre-reading set for evoking relevant prior knowledge and predicting what will happen in a story, coupled with discussion of why it is important to do so, results in even better inferential comprehension and even helps literal questions.

Story Structure

During reading comprehension, the reader continuously asks questions in order to understand the text. Teaching learners to look at the story structure is important in reading comprehension.

According to Lehr and Osborn (2005:18), the story structure is "the way the content and events of a story are organised into a plot." This is where readers ask themselves questions about various aspects of the story (NRP, 2000). In the same vein, Lehr and Osborn (2005:18) state that learners who can recognise the story structure have greater appreciation and understanding of and a memory for stories. These strategies train learners to learn to ask themselves question during reading about the basic components of stories as they read. Learners learn to identify the categories of content, namely, setting, initiating events, internal reactions, goal attempts and outcomes and how this content is organised into a plot (Lehr and Osborn, 2005:18). This implies that during teaching reading comprehension, teachers need to ask and answer five questions: Who is the main character? Where and when did the story occur? What did the main character do? How did the story end? How did the main character feel? This will help learners to learn to understand about, that is, the, who and what, where, when and why of stories. They learn to identify what happened and what was done in the story, for example, learners should recognise the story structure through the use of story maps. They also learn to identify the main character of the story, where and when the story took place, what the main character did, how the story ended, and how the main characters felt. Learners learn to construct a story map recording the setting, problem, goal, action and outcome over time (Armbruster *et al.,* 2003:11-12). A type of graphic organiser shows the sequence of events in simple stories. Instruction in the content and organisation of stories improve learners' comprehension and memory of stories.

Summarising

Another strategy that can be used in teaching reading comprehension is summarising. This requires learners to determine what is important in what they are reading, to condense information and to put it into their own words (Armbruster *et al.,* 2003:53). This implies that during reading comprehension, teachers must teach learners to read the text and synthesise the information. Routman (2000:140) refers to summarising as the ability to state the main ideas in a text in a clear and coherent manner. This involves paraphrasing and reorganising text information. It requires readers to sift through large units of text, differentiating important from unimportant ideas, and the significant from the insignificant (Armbruster *et al.,* 2003:13) and then synthesise those ideas and create a new coherent text that stands for, by substantive criteria, the original (Dole, Duffy, Roehler and Pearson, 1999:244). In the same vein, Klinger and Vaughn (1999) and the NRP (2000) maintain that summarisation can be taught effectively and that the ability to summarise can improve comprehension recall.

According to the NRP (2000), during summarising learners are taught to integrate ideas and generalise from the text information. Summarising involves identifying the main idea in a paragraph or composing a concise statement of the main concepts from a long passage; this helps learners to focus on the main ideas or and encourage learners to reread as they construct a summary (Kamil, 2004). Summarising requires learners to determine what is important in what they are reading, to condense this information, and to put it into their own words (Lehr and Osborn, 2005). In so doing, learners identify or generate main ideas, connect the main or central ideas, and remember what they read. They learn to make connections among main ideas through the text. However, "summarising sounds difficult and the research demonstrates that, in fact, it is a difficult task" (Dole *et al.,* 1999:244).

Teachers therefore need to give learners opportunities to practice the summarising strategy before they apply it. Summarising will enable learners to process the text more deeply and better retain their knowledge of the text. In teaching summarising as a strategy, teachers need to teach learners to summarise main ideas and leave out the less important aspects.

How Can Comprehension Strategies Be Taught?

Effective comprehension strategy instruction is explicit. The teacher tells readers why and when they should use strategies, what strategies to use, and how to apply them. The steps typically include an explanation of the strategy, teacher modelling, guided practice and application.

- Explanation–The teacher explains to students why the strategy helps comprehension and when to apply it.

  The teacher provided a clear explanation about the structure of the strategy to be learned and described when and how it could be used.

- Modelling–The teacher models or demonstrates how to apply the strategy, usually by "thinking aloud" while reading text that students are using.

  The teacher modelled the use of the strategy so learners were able to see how it would be used in an appropriate situation.

- Guided Practice–The teacher guides and assists students as they learn how and when to apply the strategy.

  Explicit strategy instruction was provided and applied in the context of the reading selection.

- Application–The teacher helps students practice the strategy until they can apply it independently.

  The learners were encouraged to use before, during, and after reading strategies as appropriate Reading strategy instruction moved learners toward independent use through scaffolding.

  The teacher then helps readers to use strategies flexibly and in combination with other strategies.

  Effective comprehension strategy instruction can also be accomplished through cooperative and collaborative learning. (Armbruster, Lehr and Osborn, 2001).

When Is Comprehension Instruction Most Effective?

Comprehension instruction is most effective when teachers:

- Model and think aloud their own use of the strategies.
- Provide explicit and in-depth instruction and practice of strategies over time.
- Discuss explicitly how each strategy helps readers to better comprehend text.
- Make connections between each new strategy and what the reader already knows.
- Gradually release responsibility for the use of strategies to students.
- Build in time for actual text reading and guided practice in strategy application by the students.
- Show students how each strategy applies to other texts, genres, formats, disciplines, and contexts.
- Help students notice how strategies intersect and work in conjunction with one another. (Harvey and Goudvis, 2000)

About Comprehension Strategy Instruction Teachers should take consideration of the following:

Are Learners Taught to:

- Identify the purpose of reading?
- Preview texts before reading?
- Make predictions before and during reading?
- Activate relevant background knowledge for reading?
- Think aloud when reading?
- Use text structures to support comprehension?
- Create visual representations to aid comprehension and recall?
- Determine the important ideas in what they read?
- Summarise what they read?
- Generate questions for texts?

- Handle unfamiliar words during reading?
- Monitor their comprehension during reading?

Does instruction about these strategies include:

- An explicit description of the strategy and when it should be used?
- Modelling of the strategy in action?
- Collaborative use of the strategy?
- Guided practice using the strategy, with gradual release of responsibility?
- Independent practice using the strategy?

About the teaching consideration. Teachers must consider the following suggestions

- Are learners helped to orchestrate multiple strategies, rather than using only one at a time?
- Are the texts used for instruction carefully chosen to match the strategy and learners being taught?
- Is there concern with learners' motivation to engage in literacy activities and apply strategies learned?
- Are learners' comprehension skills assessed on an ongoing basis?

Conclusion on reading comprehension

The chapter highlighted the understanding and the connection between comprehension and reading development.

It gives detailed information and suggestion on how the teacher can teach learners to Learn, while at the same time they model, and teach research-based strategies for comprehension instruction in the classroom.

It was highlighted that in order to improve the teaching of comprehension teachers must create an action plan to apply in their teaching practice.

It is important for teachers to note that by saying words is not reading and or an indication that learners do understanding the written text. It was explained that reading with comprehension requires purposeful, thoughtful, and active interactions between the reader, the text, the activity, and the socio-cultural context.

Reading comprehension is a challenge worldwide. However, there is agreement that teaching reading comprehension can enhance learners' understanding of texts. There are research-based comprehension strategies which the teacher must know and model during reading. Teachers must monitor learners' understanding and ensure that they use the strategies correctly. The literature revealed that South Africa still lacks the theoretical base to guide teachers on the subject and that more research on the subject is needed.

In this chapter, I gave an overview of the international and national contexts of the teaching of reading comprehension. I briefly discussed various strategies and their importance in teaching reading comprehension. It is evident that reading comprehension is a process. Teachers should organise their comprehension teaching in the three phases of reading lesson namely, before, during and after reading as discussed in this chapter, to help learners understand the importance and the correct use of strategies. It is clear that before teaching comprehension, teachers must first examine the text for rigour, level of questioning and vocabulary. During reading, teachers must deepen the learners' level of understanding by modelling the reading text. They must provide multiple opportunities for the learners to read and interact with the text. I explained that it is important during reading to deepen learners understanding by asking them open-ended questions at various levels and not only yes and no questions. Teachers must teach learners to read the text and be able to generate questions from the text.

Teachers must monitor learners' understanding and ensure that learners use the strategies correctly. After teaching, teachers must be able to reflect on learners' responses to instruction and plan for deeper teaching opportunities. It is clear that reading comprehension teaching needs a strategic teacher who is competent and knowledgeable, for example, the teacher must know that before reading he/she must teach learners to learn to set a purpose for reading, provide questions and connections to motivate learners to be involved in their own learning.

In addition, the teacher must pre-teach key vocabulary concepts, link learners' background knowledge and experiences relate the text to learners' lives and teach learners text features and how to use them. The same strategies may be used during and after reading, for example, the teacher must teach learners how to monitor understanding through demonstration and think aloud, provide questions to consider while reading, help them draw inferences from text, ask them to summarise the main ideas of a paragraph and to confirm, disconfirm, or extend predictions and generated questions.

Teachers have a pivotal role in helping learners to acquire these skills and preparing them for independent learning. Capacity building for teachers is therefore needed, with appropriate guidelines on how to teach reading comprehension. It is clear that comprehension is a problem-solving process. That is why it is critical for teachers to have a substantial knowledge of the strategies and how best to teach and help learners to acquire and use strategies appropriately. Indeed, teachers need to respond to the individual learners' needs and provide various reading experiences to foster their ability to use strategies correctly and progress to self-regulatory learning.

The literature review revealed that the best time to lay a strong foundation is to teach reading comprehension strategies from an early age when children start school, instead of attempting to teach them later in their school years when the harm has already been done.

Summary of teaching reading comprehension is explained in the following table

Factors relating to teachers
• Knowledge and use of various reading comprehension strategies appropriately instructional competency • School learning environment

(Contd...)

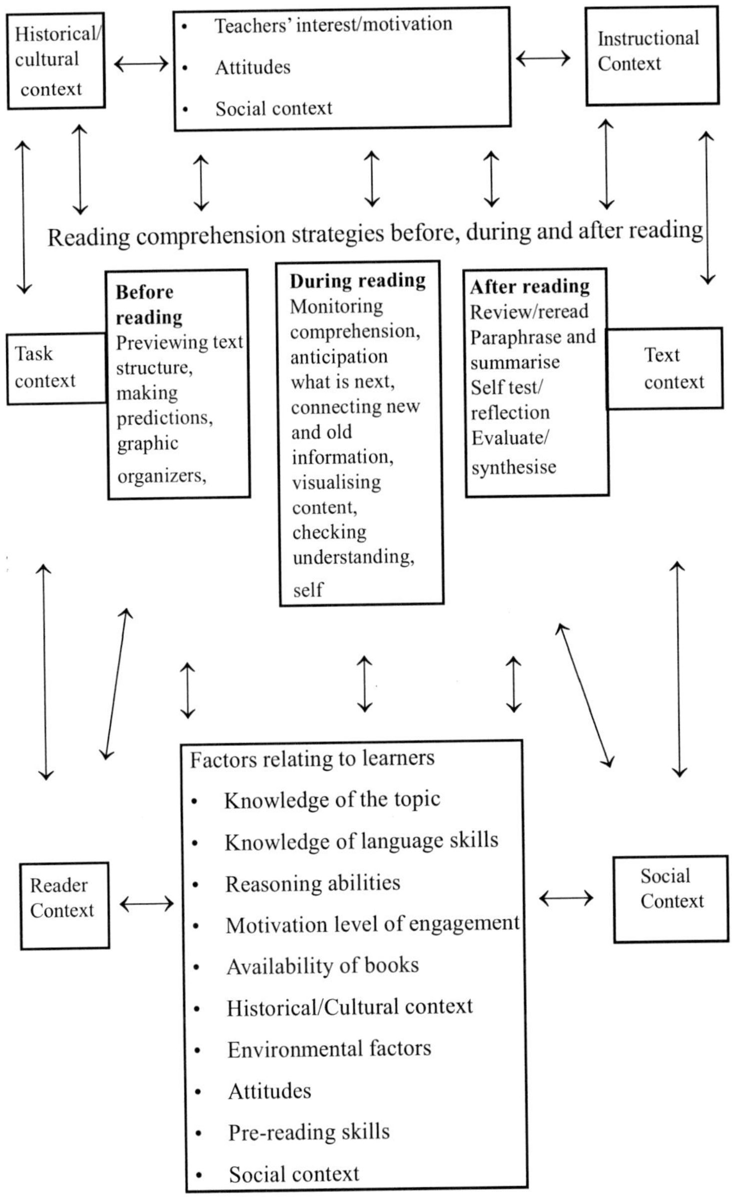

Reading comprehension

Figure 2.1 illustrates the teaching of reading comprehension. From the table above, there are several factors that contribute to the teaching of reading comprehension; these factors are interrelated- one affects the other and they were discussed. It is therefore important that parties, the teacher and the learner take responsibility of his/her own task.

From the figure above, teachers must learn the strategies in order to interact with learners at the right time and right place during the reading of the text. Teachers must know about cognitive processes in reading and how to teach strategies before reading, during reading and after reading of the text.

In this study the quote of Pardo, (2004:272) apply:

> *"Once teachers understand what is involved in comprehending and how the factors of reader, text, and context interact to create meaning, they can more easily teach their students to be effective comprehenders. That there is a great need to know just how much of an impact on reading achievement can be made by instruction, rich in all the individual components that increase comprehension. Of course the hope is that there will be much benefit; the fear is that such instruction might be so over whelmingly complex. If all the components are simply thrown into the mix, instruction will be confusing and effective. With some experience in an attempting to mix the components, how to create more effective teaching occurs. There is much interesting work ahead before comprehension instruction is understood fully".*

This implies that teachers must be competent and clear about the use of strategies. The teacher must demonstrate such strategy for the learners and provide many opportunities for learners to use the strategy until the learners can be able to use them independently.

Chapter - 4

Teaching Vocabulary

Learners develop vocabulary in reading as they learn the meaning of new words. The greater a learner's vocabulary the more likely the learners will comprehend what he or she reads. Learners develop and refine their vocabulary through listening to stories being read and through the process of actually reading (Yatvin,Weaver and Garan, 2003). Studies that demonstrate that successful learners are those who apply a variety of strategies and this contribute to their success in language skills and vocabulary. The ability to recognise and decode words is critical to mastering the reading of print. Learners with limited vocabulary will have difficulty with comprehension. Obviously they may know very few words on a page, unless the text is very simple (Westwood, 2001).Teachers must know which method; strategies that will best suite best the level of their learners in class. It is critical for teachers to know and teach these strategies to their learners. Both L1 and L2 researchers agree that good language learners are good because they have better ways of handling their problems in the learning process when need arise.

Vocabulary is not a one skill that can be taught in various ways. According to Smith (2003, 2), there are four levels of vocabulary proficiency namely, listening vocabulary, reading vocabulary, writing vocabulary and speaking vocabulary. All these levels are critical for the development of vocabulary skills.

However, there is not one method to teach vocabulary. Smith (2003:2-3) identifies three factors that affect the methods of teaching vocabulary.

Active processing. This is when learners are doing something with a word more than just parroting the definition; they are more likely to remember that word.

Different contexts: we can learn much about a word's meaning through different contexts in which it is used. The more different contexts we encounter with the word, the more flexible we become with that word and its meaning and the more likely it is that will remember it.

Using several techniques for reviewing that word instead of only one: just as learners acquire vocabulary more readily through encountering words in varying contexts, varying kinds of review activities apparently enhance vocabulary development. Each review activity reveals a word and its meaning in a different way, offering its own perspective on the word and its meaning.

Learning and Language Strategies

Learning strategies are defined as "specific action, behaviours, steps, or techniques–such as seeking out conversation partners, or giving oneself encouragement to tackle a difficult language task–used by students to enhance their own learning" (Scarcella and Oxford, 1992: 63). In other words, they are mental a communicative procedure learner use in order to learn and use a language (Nunan, 1991). When the learner consciously chooses strategies that fit his or her learning style and the L2 task at hand, these strategies become a useful toolkit for active, conscious, and purposeful self-regulation of learning.

Language learning strategies has been classified by many scholars (Wenden and Rubin, 1987; O'Malley *et al.,* 1985; Oxford, 1990; Stern, 1992; Ellis, 1994). For example, Rubin (1987) classified language learning strategies as learning strategies, communication strategies and social strategies. Oxford (1990: 9) divides language learning strategies into two main classes, direct and indirect. The former consists of memory, cognitive and compensation strategies while the latter includes metacognitive, affective and social strategies. However, Oxford's classification of learning strategies is somewhat complicated and confusing as she treats compensation strategies as a direct type of learning strategies and memory strategies as separate ones from cognitive strategies.

According to Stern (1992:262-266), there are five main language learning strategies. These are management and planning strategies, cognitive strategies, communicative–Experiential strategies, interpersonal strategies, affective strategies.

The framework that has been most useful and generally accepted is O'Malley and Chamot (1990)'s. In O'Malley and Chamot's framework, three major types of strategies named as metacognitive, cognitive and social/ affective are distinguished in accordance with the information processing model, on which their research is based. The subtypes of these strategies were identifies by O'Malley and Chamot on the basis of their several descriptive studies on learning strategies used by second language learners (see Table 1).

According to Oxford (1990:8), learning strategies as "learning strategies are specific actions taken by the learner to make learning easier, faster, more enjoyable, more self-directed, more effective and more transferable to new situations." In this view the learner is not passive but has to be actively involved in their learning. In addition, Oxford pointed that the importance of learning strategies is that they improve proficiency and greater self-confidence in learners. The learner is confident because when the need arise he/she knows which strategy to use. As a result, then learning becomes more enjoyable.

Different researchers have their own views and opinions in defining language learning strategies. Language learning strategies are defined as "techniques which learners use to comprehend, store and remember information and skills" (Chamot and Kupper, 1989:9).

There is a interrelationship between language learning strategies and vocabulary learning strategies. According to (Nation, 2001, Schmitt,1997), language learning strategies (LLS) form the sub-class of learning strategies in general whereas vocabulary learning strategies (VLS) constitute a sub-class of language learning strategies.

So because of the interrelationship both the LLS and the VLS will be discussed in this paper. In the same vein, researchers O'Malley and Chamot, (1990) and Oxford (1990) confirmed that VLS form a subclass of framework for language learning strategies and that for this reason are applicable for to a wide variety of language learning (LL) tasks. In essence, the vast majority of language learning strategies listed in taxonomy of Oxford, 1990 are either vocabulary learning strategies or can be used for vocabulary learning task such as, sighting from more remote ones, such as vocabulary, pronunciation and grammar in order to integrative task. These include such as reading comprehension and oral communication. In this paper I reviewed language learning strategies which include vocabulary learning strategies. This is because in learning any language vocabulary becomes crucial and therefore it should be taught and learnt hence learning strategies.

Oxford (1990:9) highlight that features of LLS contribute to the goal of communicative competence, allow learners to become more self-directed, expand the role of teachers, are problem-oriented, specific actions taken by the learner, involve many aspects of the learner, not just cognitive, support learning both directly and indirectly, are not always observable, are often conscious, can be taught, are flexible and are influenced by a variety of factors.

The Importance of Strategies in the Learning Process

Knowledge of strategies is important because if one is conscious of the processes underlying the learning that he/she is involved in, then the learning will be more effective. The fact showed that learners who are taught learning strategies are more highly motivated than those who are not. However, not all learners automatically know which strategies work best for them. For this reason, explicit strategy training, coupled with thinking about how one goes about learning, and experimenting with different strategies, can lead to more effective learning. Oxford (1990: 1) argues that strategies are important for two reasons. In the first place, strategies "...are tools for active, self-directed involvement, which is essential for developing communicative competence". Secondly, learners who have developed appropriate learning strategies have greater self-confidence and learn more effectively. In her book, she identifies twelve key features of strategies. According to Oxford, language learning strategies:

- Contribute to the main goal, communicative competence.
- Allow learners to become more self-directed.
- Expand the role of teachers.
- Support learning both directly and indirectly.
- Vocabulary instruction can be either direct or indirect. This module will focus on direct instruction. Direct vocabulary instruction occurs when a teacher systematically demonstrates how to determine the meanings of words by utilising contextual and conceptual clues. Although students learn the words in the context of authentic reading, the teacher leads them to specific strategies for discovering meaning.
- Indirect vocabulary instruction involves exposing students to a wide variety of literary sources. In her book *Words, Words, Words*, Janet Allen writes, "They used the words they heard on television and radio; they used words from the music they listened to; and they used the words I used with them." Vocabulary growth occurs naturally when students read, write, talk, and listen to each other on a daily basis. When in a rich literary environment, such as a classroom, students internalise the language used in meaningful contexts.

1. Strategies in Teaching Second Language Reading

Reading comprehension strategies are seen as comprehension processes that enable readers to construct meaning from the printed page most effectively. In other words, those strategies show how readers tackle a reading task, how they interpret their reading and what they do when they do not comprehend.

Many researchers have similarities in categorising reading strategies. For example, Anderson (1999), Brantmeier (2002), Almasi (2003) and Sugirin (1999) emphasised the role of prior knowledge in reading. Brantmeier (2002) and Brown (1990) introduced skimming, scanning and guessing as effective strategies in reading. However, there are some differences in their classification.

For instance, Brantmeier (2002: 1) summarises reading strategies as follows:

> *"the strategies may involve skimming, scanning, guessing, recognising cognates and word families, reading for meaning, predicting, activating general knowledge, making inferences, following references, and separating main ideas from supporting ideas".*

Furthermore, reading strategies can consist of evaluating content, such as ageing or disagreeing, making an association with prior knowledge or experience, asking and answering questions, looking at the key words, using sentence structure analysis such as determining the subject, verb, or object of the sentence, skipping and rereading (Almasi, 2003; Sugirin, 1999). Clearly, not all strategies are of equal effectiveness due to the different types of reading texts and tasks, and reading strategy use by each reader.

Brown (1990: 3) provides strategies that can help students read more quickly and effectively:

- *Previewing:* reviewing titles, section headings and photo captions to get a sense of the structure and content of a reading selection.
- *Predicting:* using knowledge of the subject matter to make predictions about content and vocabulary and check comprehension, using knowledge of the text type and purpose to make predictions about discourse structure, using knowledge about the author to make predictions about writing style, vocabulary and content.
- *Skimming and scanning:* using a quick survey of the text to get the main idea, identify text structure, confirm or question predictions.
- *Guessing from context:* using prior knowledge of the subject and the ideas in the text as clues to the meanings of unknown words, instead of stopping to look them up.
- *Paraphrasing:* stopping at the end of a selection to check comprehension by restarting the information and ideas in the text.

Anderson (1999: 4) introduces six strategies for consideration when teaching reading:

A. Activate prior knowledge

C. Cultivate vocabulary

T. Teach for comprehension

A. Increase reading rate

V. Verify reading strategies

E. Evaluate progress

Effective language instructors show students how they can adjust their reading behaviour to deal with a variety of situations, types of input, and reading purposes. They help students develop a set of reading strategies and match appropriate strategies situation.

In addition, these strategies appear to be effective since they help language learners enhance the reading ability.

A number of researchers have proposed several classification of language learning strategies in many ways, some differently and some in the same ways. For example, Rubin (1981) and Oxford (1990) classified language learning strategies into two broad categories namely, direct and indirect strategies which were subdivided into six categories groups. However, Oxford suggested a list of strategies under each of the two broad categories namely, direct strategies include memory strategies, cognitive strategies and compensation strategies. Indirect strategies include metacognitive strategies, affective strategies and social strategies.

According to Oxford, direct and indirect strategies support each other and they function as a mutual support network within which various types of strategies assist the learners to improve the language. It should be noted that Oxford grounded her classification framework based on the theory that learners are made up of social, emotional, intellectual, physical and therefore learners must viewed as whole person and not part.

According to Oxford and Crookall (1990:404) the following is the definition of each strategy category:

1. **Direct strategies.**

   These strategies are important because they are directly involved and deal with the target language. They include the following sub-strategies:

   1.1 *Memory strategies.* These are techniques specifically tailored to help learners to store new information and retrieve it later. For example, grouping, imagery, rhyming or moving.

   1.2 *Cognitive strategies.* These are skills that involve manipulation or transformation of the language material in direct ways. For example, reasoning, analysis, note taking, summarising and practicing in naturalistic settings.

   1.3 *Compensation strategies.* These are behaviours used to compensate for missing knowledge of some kind. For example guessing meanings from context and using synonyms and gestures to convey meaning.

2. **Indirect strategies**

   These are important strategies that support and manage language learning. They include the following sub-strategies:

   2.1 *Metacognitive strategies.* These are behaviours used for centering, arranging, planning and evaluating one's learning. For example, evaluating one's progress, planning for language tasks, consciously searching for practice opportunities.

   2.2 *Social strategies.* These are actions involving other people in the language learning process. For example, questioning, cooperating with peers.

   2.3 *Affective strategies.* These are techniques which help learners to gain better control over their emotions, motivations and attitudes related to language learning. For example, reducing anxiety, self-encouragement and self-reward.

Table 1: Learning Strategy Definition and Classification (O' Malley and Chamot, 1990: 119

Learning strategies	*Definition*
A. Metacognitive Strategies **Planning**	
Advance Organisers	Previewing the main ideas and concepts of the material to be learned, often by skimming the text for the organising principle.
Directed attention	Deciding in advance to attend in general to a learning task and to ignore irrelevant distracters.
Functional planning	Planning for and rehearing linguistic components necessary to carry out an upcoming task.
Selective attention	Deciding in advance to attend to specific aspects of input, often by scanning for key words, concepts and/ or linguistic markers.
Self-management	Understanding the conditions that help one learn and arranging for the presence of those conditions.
Monitoring	
Self-monitoring	Checking one's comprehension during listening or reading checking the accuracy and/ or appropriateness of one's oral or written production while it is talking place.
Evaluation	
Self-evaluation	Checking the outcomes of one's own language against a standard after it has been completed.
B. Cognitive Strategies	
Resourcing	Using target language reference material such as dictionaries, encyclopaedias, or textbooks.
Repetition	Imitating a language model, including overt practice and silent rehearsal.
Grouping	Classifying words, terminology or concepts according to the attributes or meaning.
Deduction	Applying rules to understand or produce the second language making up rules based on language analysis.
Imagery	Using visual images (either mental or actual) to under stand or remember new information.
Auditory representation	Planning back in one's mind the sound of word, phrase or longer language sequence.
Key word method	Remember a new word in the second language by: (1) identifying a familiar word in the first language

(Contd...)

	that sounds like or otherwise resembles the new word, and (2) generating easily recalled images of some relationship with the first language homonym and the new word in the second language.
Elaboration	Relating new information to prior knowledge, relating different parts of new information to each other, or making meaningful personal associations with the new information.
Transfer	Using previous linguistic knowledge or prior skills to assist comprehension or production.
Inferencing	Using available information to guess meaning of new items, predict outcomes or fill in missing information.
Note taking	Writing down key words or concepts in abbreviated verbal, graphic or numerical form while listening or reading.
Summarising	Making a mental, oral written summary of new information gained through listening or reading.
Recombination	Constructing a meaningful sentence or larger language sequence by combining known elements in a new way.
Translation	Using the first language as a base for understanding and/or producing the second language.
C. Social/Affective Strategies	
Question for clarification	Eliciting from a teacher or peer additional explanations, rephrasing, examples or verification.
Cooperation	Working together with one or more peers to solve a problem, pool information, check a learning task, model a language activity, or get feedback on oral or written performance.
Self-talk	Reducing anxiety by using mental techniques that makes one feel competent to do the learning task.

Vocabulary Learning Strategies (VLS)

There is evidence that the relationship is largely reciprocal. "The good news for teachers from research in vocabulary development is that vocabulary instruction does improve reading comprehension" (Stahl,1999). Vocabulary learning strategies are knowledge about the mechanisms (process, strategies) used to learn vocabulary as well as specific actions or mental operations taken by learners to (to find out the meaning of unknown words, (b) retain them in long-term memory (recall them at will and (d) use them in oral or written mode (Catala'n, 2003:56). The National Reading Panel (2000) clearly finding that vocabulary learning strategies is a necessary and important factor in primary grades and can have long-term effects. These findings suggest that primary teachers may be able to help narrow, or halt the widening gap of word knowledge through explicit teaching of vocabulary by using VLS and VI effectively. Therefore, teachers should have knowledge base of the research-based strategies and how to employ them.

As in language learning strategies several researchers classified vocabulary learning strategies in many ways. For example, Gu and Johnson (1996) classified vocabulary learning strategies into seven categories namely, metacognitive regulation, guessing strategies, dictionary strategies, note-taking strategies, rehearsal strategies, encoding strategies and activation strategies. However, in order to address this gap, Schmitt (1997) proposed a taxonomy of vocabulary learning strategies (VLS) which are divided into two broad categories namely, discovery and consolidation strategies. These two broad categories were sub-divided into five subcategories namely, determination, social, memory, cognitive and metacognitive strategies. Social strategies were included in both categories. According to Schmitt are found in both because they can be used for both discovery and determination purposes. Each is discussed below.

Determination/Discovery Strategies (DET)

Discovery strategies include several determination strategies and social strategies. A learners may discover a new word's meaning through guessing from context, guessing or by asking someone else. According to Schmitt (1997:205-206), all strategies employed to discovery activities could be used as consolidation strategies. This can be used in the learners' later stage of vocabulary learning.

Strategies for the discovery of a new word include strategies of determination which are used by an individual when facing with discovery a new word's meaning without recourse to another person's expertise. Determination strategies facilitate gaining knowledge of a new word by means of guessing from any available information and from mother tongue, texts, and consulting reference materials such as dictionary, word list and flashcards.

Guessing through Context

In order to succeed, Nation (2001), Schmitt, (1997) found that incidental learning via guessing from context is the most important of all sources of vocabulary learning. This shows that vocabulary learning can happen within a social context which may tends to be more interpreted as simple textual context. In addition, knowledge of the subject being read, or knowledge of the conceptual structure of the topic should also be taken into consideration (Yu-Ling, (2005).

Dictionary Use

Another vocabulary strategy that is important in vocabulary learning is the using of dictionary. A dictionary can be used in both a receptive and a productive skill in language learning. However, the disadvantage of dictionary use is that learners hardly have time to use the dictionary and in indigenous languages learners do not have a dictionary. Teachers help learners to develop a so called dictionary by writing new words in the book. But this does not serve as a dictionary. Scholfield (1982:185) maintained that looking for a word in a dictionary is far from performing a purely mechanical operation. Instead, a proficient dictionary user is often required to formulate and pursue several hypotheses and make use of prior knowledge of various sorts, especially information derived from context the advantage of the dictionary as a tool to enhance vocabulary (Scholfield, 1982:185). Except for locating the unknown word in the alphabetic list, which seems to be the skill most dealt with in respect of training dictionary use, other important facets involving effective dictionary use receive little attention Scholfield (1982). Since many lexical terms in a language have more than one meaning, learners should be instructed how to reduce multiple options by elimination. Scanning all of the definitions in the entry before deciding which is the one that fits is a good idea proposed by Underhill (1980). After choosing a seemingly reasonable sense from the definitions in the entry, a user then needs to understand the definition and integrate it into the context where the unknown was met Scholfield (1982:190). The most sophisticated parts involving dictionary use arise when none of the senses in the entry seems to fit the context or more than one fits. In these situations, a user may need to infer a meaning that comes from the senses in the entry or seek further contextual clues in the source text to disambiguate Scholfield (1982:193). Each of the above skills may be practiced separately through well-designed activities and only in this way can effective dictionary use be maximised and misunderstanding minimised.

Word Part Analysis

Word part analysis is important in helping learners to learn both high frequency and low frequency words (Nation, 2001). Firstly, learners need to be able to recognise prefixes and suffixes so that they may break unknown word into parts. Secondly, they need to relate the meaning of the word parts to the dictionary meaning of the word. To achieve this goal, learners have to know the meanings of the common word parts and to be able to re-express the dictionary definition of a word to include the meaning of its prefix and if possible, its stem and suffix (Nation, 2001:278).

The second category of vocabulary strategies is the consolidation strategies.

Consolidation Strategies

What are consolidation strategies?

After the learners has been introduced to a new word, he/she need to make some effort to consolidate or remember the word by using social, memory, cognitive and metacognitive strategies. Consolidation strategies include the following categories.

1.3.2.1 Social strategies (SOC) which use interaction with other people to find out a new word's meaning.

Vocabulary learning is a social concept. Teachers must provide learners with an opportunity to interact with the others. Social strategies involve disobeying a new word's meaning by asking someone else who knows such as classmates or by discussing during small group work. Teachers can be helpful to the learners by translating.

Memorisation Strategies (MEM)

Memorisation strategies refer to those strategies involved in making connections between the to-be-learned word and some previously learned knowledge, using some form of imagery or grouping. Memorisation strategies play an important role in helping learners to commit new words into memory and in the whole process of vocabulary learning. These strategies according to Schmitt, 1997: 213 can have long-term retention.

In his taxonomy of VLS Schmitt, 1997 includes 27 memorisation strategies which can enhance vocabulary learning. According to Schimitt, learners can learn to memorise words by using techniques such as study word with pictorial representation of its meaning, associate the word with its coordinates, use semantic maps, group words together within a story line through Peg Method or Loci Method, group words together by colour, size, function, likes/dislikes, or any other feature that makes sense, they can paraphrase a word's meaning, use multi-word chunks (phases or idioms, or put the words in a meaningful context (sentences or story lines), or explicitly study a word's spelling or pronunciation, study the grammatical or morphological aspect of a word, use cognates or physical actions to aid recall, study the spelling of a word, use Keyword method, use physical action when learning a words. Researchers, (Pressley *et al.*, 1982) indicated that the Keyword method is an effective method of improving retrieval. The Keyword Method involves learner finding a L1 word which sounds like the target L2 word and creating an image combining the two concepts (Nation, 1990).

Cognitive Strategies (COG)

These strategies exhibit the common function of manipulation or transformation of the target language learner. Researchers, Lin, 2001; Fowle, 2002, Schmitt and Schmitt,1995 indicate the advantage of the cognitive strategies as to enhance vocabulary acquisition. According to Schmitt, 1997 taxonomy, cognitive strategies are similar to memory strategies. However, they are not focused specifically on manipulative mental processing. Cognitive strategies refer to written and verbal repetition as well as some mechanical means involving vocabulary learning. Whereas mechanical means involve taking notes in class or making use of study aids such as word list, flash cards, vocabulary sections in text books, labelling physical objects, tapes of word lists and vocabulary notebooks.

Metacognitive Strategies (MET)

Metacognitive strategies are broad and concerned with more efficient learning (Schmitt,1997:216).These strategies involve conscious overview of the learning process and making decisions about planning, monitoring, or evaluating the best ways to study (Lin, 2001). The study of Gu and Johnson (1996) has found that metacognitive strategies pay an important role in language learning. Within the metacognitive strategies teachers should train learners to control and evaluate their own learning through various ways Schmitt, 1997. For example, using spaced word practice, continuing to study word overtime, self-testing. Metacognitive strategies include strategies such as when learners take the decision to skip or pass a new words when it is judged to be allow frequency one which may not be met again for a long time.

Researchers (Daniels and Zamelman, 2004) indicate that vocabulary instruction is a necessary and important factor in primary reading instruction and can have long-term effects. These findings clearly confirmed that vocabulary learning is a more complex process and that it involves seeing, hearing and using words in a meaningful way (Daniels and Zamelman, 2004:13).

According to Graves (2006) and Christ and Wang (2010) an effective and comprehensive primary vocabulary programme should contain four components. It is important for teachers to support children in their classrooms. Christ and Wang (2010:86-87) identified four research-based vocabulary teaching practices that teachers can support young children in the teaching of vocabulary instruction. These include provide purposeful exposure to new words, intentionally teach word meanings, teach word learning strategies and offer opportunities to use newly learned words. Each will be discussed.

Rich Varied Language Experiences

Listening and speaking in grades K-3 are the primary ways teachers can promote vocabulary growth. Immersing students in a variety of rich language experiences that allow learners to learn words through listening, speaking, reading and writing is key to an effective vocabulary programme. Most of the new words primary grades children learn come from listening and discussion. Teachers of primary grades need to directly build their learners oral vocabularies through interactive oral reading (Graves, 2006). Effective interactive reading includes:

- Using interesting and enjoyable books for children.
- Having adults read with expression to engage children.
- Reading books several times.
- Focusing children's attention to a small number of words.
- Interaction of the reader and children as they discuss and ask questions about the text (Graves, 2006).

Teaching Individual Words

There is an overwhelming quantity of words learners need to learn. Teachers cannot teach all of them directly in a school year, but that does not mean they should not teach some of them. Not every word a teacher wants to introduce to learners from a text requires rich instruction and knowledge. Context can give enough information about some words to acquire and maintain meaning. Rich instruction is needed only for words that are necessary for comprehension of the text or that turn up in a wide variety of contexts, or that require more than a brief explanation to be understood (McKeown and Beck, 2004). The experts (Beck *et al.,* 2002; Graves, 2006; Nagy, 1988) agree on the following effective ways to teach a new word:

- Use a definition of the word and have students work with the word in context.
- Have learners actively relate similarities and differences of a new word to words and concepts they know and practice using the word in various situations.
- Provide multiple exposures to a new word through games, definitions and using it orally and/or in writing.
- Review and remind learners about the word as it occurs in other contexts over time.
- Spend time learning the word.

Effective word learning instruction provides examples of a word used in various contexts and includes discussion what the word means in each context. Children need contextual and definitional information to gain understanding of how the meaning of a word changes in different contexts (Stahl, 2003; Stahl and Fairbanks, 1986).

Juel and Deffes (2004) conducted a six-week study with kindergarten learners comparing three forms of vocabulary instruction-context-based, anchored word and analytic vocabulary instruction. The teachers using the context-based method related word meanings to the background knowledge of the learners. The analytic word method had learners analyse word meanings along with connecting the word to background knowledge. The anchored word method had learners analysing words, connecting words to background knowledge and focusing on the letters and sounds of the words. All of the instruction was delivered through storybook reading where five words were targeted from each book. The study found the analytic and anchored methods were the most effective in teaching word meanings to learners. There was not a significant difference between the two methods. The study did find that learners who were behind their peers in letter- naming fluency seemed to make greater gains in vocabulary growth if they had received the anchored method of instruction (Juel and Deffes, 2004).

Teaching Word Learning Strategies

The use of word learning strategies can increase vocabulary acquisition. A teacher cannot teach every word his or her learners will encounter, but by teaching word learning strategies, a teacher can help learners become independent word learners (Blachowicz and Fisher, 2006; Graves, 2006; Nagy, 1988). Three important word-learning strategies are: (1) teaching learners to use context to infer the meanings of unknown words, (2) teaching students to use word parts to glean word meanings, and (3) teaching learners to use the dictionary (Graves, 2006:23). In addition Christ and Wang (2010:86) suggested that teachers must teach learners how to do it. While reading aloud teachers should follow the three steps. Firstly, the teacher must model how to use clues and background knowledge to infer word meaning several times; secondly, teachers must ask learners questions to guide them through the same process many times and thirdly the teacher must ask learners to infer word meanings independently and the clues in the text.

Primary teachers can informally begin to teach these strategies through modelling, scaffolding and discussion with their learners. More formal teaching of word learning strategies should occur in grade 4 and above (Graves, 2006). Lubliner and Smetana's book, *Getting Into Words:* vocabulary *instruction that Strengthens Comprehension* (2005), dedicates a chapter to teaching word learning strategies in the primary grade. The goal of a primary teacher is to help learners be aware of words they do not know and decide if the word is important to the meaning of the text. This metacognitive approach to word learning encourages learners to think about the unknown word, determine if they have heard it before, try to find the word's meaning from the rest of the sentence or paragraph, and look at the parts of the word in order to determine the meaning. This process is most often taught informally through shared storybook reading (Lubliner and Smetana, 2005).

Fostering Word Consciousness

Word consciousness is an effective way to facilitate learner's vocabulary development (Christ and Wang, 2010). "Word consciousness refers to the knowledge and dispositions necessary for learners to learn, appreciate, and effectively use words" (Scott and Nagy, 2004). When a child is word conscious, they have an interest in and an awareness of words around them- words they read, hear, speak and write (Graves, 2006). Word consciousness is not another component of vocabulary instruction, but rather the goal teachers strive for their learners to attain as they teach individual words, word-learning strategies and provide rich language experiences (Scott and Nagy, 2004).

To foster word consciousness, a teacher must model and encourage an enthusiasm for new words. The use of games, riddles, homophones, and puzzles is highly motivating in primary classrooms. Reading instruction in primary grade is not just teaching students that printed words convey meaning, but that words can feel and sound good and can incite laughter and be fun to play with (Blachowicz and Fisher, 2006; Graves and Watts-Taffe, 2002). Acording to Christ and Wang (2010), there are three main approaches to directly teaching learners' word meanings. These include (1) eliciting-type of questions: to evoke learners thinking about word meanings. For example, teachers can ask them questions to elicit recognition of a vocabulary word. The advantages of using eliciting-type of questions to the learners is that they learn more word meanings than simply exposed to words in context (Senachal,1997). During this exercise teachers can also ask learners questions that request information about the concept represented by the vocabulary word (Justice, 2002); (2) Embedded definitions: embedded definitions is when teachers explain the word meanings quickly to the learners when learners encounter unfamiliar words (Christ and Wang, 2010). The reason is that the explanation of the word explained by the teacher is embedded in the natural context in which the word occurs; (3) extended instruction (multistep approach). Learners learn more about word meanings from extended instruction than embedded instruction or exposure alone (Silverman, 2007). Teachers use extended instruction when they want to help learners develop a nuanced understanding of a word teachers use (Silverman, 2007). Researchers Beck, McKeown and Kucan, (2002 cited in Christ and Wang, 2010:88) suggest the steps to be implemented after read aloud exercise namely, contextualise the word as it appears in the story; explain the word's meaning; ask the learners to repeat the word aloud to create a phonological imprint; offer examples that extend beyond the story context; have learners demonstrate word-meaning understanding by making judgement, articulating an example and so on and have learners restate the word to reinforce its phonological imprint.

> *Teaching word meanings should be a way for students to define their world, to move from light to dark, to a more fine-grained description of the colours that surround us.*—Steven Stahl (1999)

In a study of vocabulary learning, Beck *et al.* (1982) found that students in one particular middle school classroom learned more incidental vocabulary (words that had not been taught) than the other classrooms. Researchers, attempting to find the cause, found a poster of interesting words in the classroom. The teacher stated it was the class "word wall." Whenever a student encountered a new word from TV, conversation or reading, they could write the word on the poster and share where they heard or saw it. The students received points in a class contest when they used the new word. This simple activity fostered word consciousness by motivating students to look and listen for new words and use them in their speech and writing. Teachers play a vital role in helping their students become word conscious.

When teachers use rich vocabulary in the classrooms, teach words fully so that their students can develop new word schemas and create an environment where students can explore and use words, they are giving their students tools necessary for success in school and beyond (Scott and Nagy, 2004).

There are endless ways to teach and practice vocabulary. The following are some of Research evidenced-based vocabulary instruction techniques:

Incorporate a Word of the Day in your Do It Now
Create a Word Wall of vocabulary words that students encounter as they read
Have students keep word journals of interesting or unknown words as they read
Use pre-reading strategies to introduce new words and make predictions about their meaning
Utilise Graphic Organisers such as semantic maps
Teach word parts, such as suffixes, prefixes, and roots
Ask students to create their own crossword puzzles or hangman games using vocabulary
Create a Word Sort of new vocabulary terms
Provide synonyms and antonyms of vocabulary terms
Play vocabulary Bingo
Visualise words by drawing pictures or finding pictures of vocabulary terms online or in magazines (Stacey L. Smith, Jessica L. Hoskins, and Erica Perez Spring, 2010).

Conclusion

Vocabulary knowledge is critical for success of the learners. It is therefore important that teachers of young children must help learners to develop a large word bank. This should be coupled with the teaching of effective vocabulary learning strategies. This may include explicit and implicit vocabulary instruction.

Appendices

Here are the views of some researchers about the bottom-up reading model:

Leonard Bloomfield:

- The first task of reading is learning the code or the alphabetic principle by which "written marks...conventionally represent...phonemes." (Bloomfield and Barnhart, 1961)
- The meaning of the text is expected to come naturally as the code is broken based on the reader's prior knowledge of words, their meanings, and the syntactical patterns of his/her language. (McCormick, T. 1988)
- Writing is merely a device for recording speech. (Bloomfield and Barnhart, 1961)

Emerald Dechant:

- "Bottom-up models operate on the principle that the written text is hierarchically organised (i.e., on the grapho-phonic, phonemic, syllabic, morphemic, word, and sentence levels) and that the reader first processes the smallest linguistic unit, gradually compiling the smaller units to decipher and comprehend the higher units (e.g., sentence syntax)." (Dechant, 1991)

Charles Fries:

- The reader must learn to transfer from the auditory signs for language signals...to a set of visual signs for the same signals. (Fries, 1962)
- The reader must learn to automatically respond to the visual patterns. The cumulative comprehension of the meanings signalled then enable the reader to supply those portions of

the signals which are not in the graphic representations themselves. (Fries, 1962)

- Learning to read...means developing a considerable range of habitual responses to a specific set of patterns of graphic shapes. (Fries, 1962)

Philip B Gough:

- Reading is a strictly serial process: letter-by-letter visual analysis, leading to positive recognition of every word through phonemic encoding. (McCormick, T. 1988)
- Lexical, syntactic and semantic rules are applied to the phonemic output which itself has been decoded from print. (McCormick, T. 1988)

Characteristics of Successful and Unsuccessful Readers

Characteristics of successful readers	Characteristics of unsuccessful readers
Use of context clues (Kahmi,1989)	Failure to use context
Word recognition through knowledge of sound, common letter sequences (Ehri,1992)	Deficient in rapid word identification (Torgesen, 2000)
Knowledge of vocabulary; good readers have extensive vocabularies (Taylor, 2000)	Weak language and metalanguage skills-vocabulary,verbal memory, semantic and syntactic cues (Torgesen, 2000)
Phonic knowledge; phonic skill represents the most powerful tool to help children become independent readers (Rubin, 2000)	Weak phonic skill
Phonological awareness-ability to understand sound features of language helps children develop 'word concept' (Adams, Treiman and Presseley, 1998)	Poor phonological awareness-therefore limited functional sight vocabulary (Gunning, 2001)
Metacognitive skills-knowledge of when to engage cognitive abilities in reading (Taylor, graves and van Den broek, 2000)	Poor metacognitive skills so fail to check purpose for reading, make predictions about text, self question as they read (Barchers, 1998).
An effective reader needs 'an understanding of the reading process and understanding of how to go about reading different types of printed information' (Wassman and Rrinsky (1993: 5), a second or foreign learner can practice technique that will help to succeed in becoming an effective reader. Besides, they also point out two necessary ingredients for an effective reader, i.e. the willingness to practice.	

Factors helping second or foreign language readers to become effective:

- *Organise properly for reading and study:* this requirements forces the reader to understand the importance of disciplined study so that they can appropriately time to devote to reading and study.
- *Improve the concentration:* actually concentration is important to learning in general and learning in particular for the fact that readers need to comprehend the printed information.
- *Maintain confidence:* confident reading is chiefly the result of preparation.

  Without this, readers can't become effective readers.

List of References

Aarnoutse, C. and Schellings, G. 2003. Learning Reading Strategies by Triggering Reading Motivation, *Educational Studies*, 29(4): 389-409.

Adler, C.R. 2004. Seven Strategies to Teach Students Texts Comprehension. Online Available: www.readingrockets.org/article/3479/.Retrieved: 12 October 2011.

Address by the Minister of Education, Naledi Pandor MP, at the Foundation Phase Conference.Online Available: http://www.education.gov.za. Retrieved: 15 March 2010.

Afflerbach, P., Pearson, P.D. and Paris, S.G. 2008.Clarifying Differences between Reading Skills and Reading Strategies,*The Reading Teacher*, 61:364-373.

Alfassi, M.2004. Reading to Learn: Effects of Combined Strategy Instruction on High School Students,*The Journal of Educational Research*, 97(4): 171-184.

Alexander, P.A., Jetton, T.l. and Kulikowich, J.M. 1995. Interrelationship of Knowledge, Interest, and Recall: Assessing a Model of Domain Learning, *Journal of Educational Psychology,* 87(4): 559-575.

Allen, S. 2003. An Analytic Comparison of Three Models of Reading Strategy instruction, *International Review of Applied Linguistics in Language Teaching*, 41(4):319-338.

Allington, R.L. 2001.*What Really Matters to Struggling Readers*. New York: Longman.

Anastasiou, D. and Griva, E. 2009. Awareness of Reading Strategy use and Reading Comprehension among Poor and Good Readers, *Elementary Education Online*, 8(20): 283-297.

Anderson, B. 1991. *Imagined Communities: Reflections on the Origin and Spread of Nationalism (Revised and Enlarged Edition)*. London: Verso.

Anderson, N.J. 2002. The Role of Metacognition in Second Language Teaching and Learning, *ERIC Digest*, April 2002:3-4.

Andreassen, R and Braten, I. 2011. Implementation and Effects of Explicit Reading Comprehension Instruction in Fifth-grade Classrooms: Learning and Instruction 21(92011): 520-537.

Antunez, B. 2002. Implementing Reading First with English Language Learners (Directions with Language and Education No. 15).Washington: George Washington University, National Clearinghouse for English Language Acquisition and Language Instruction Educational Programs. Online Available: www.ncela.gwu.edu/pubs/directions.15pdf.Retrieved: 21 June 2010.

Armbruster, B.B., Lehr, F. and Osborn, J. 2003.*Kindergarten through to Grade 3: Put Reading First: The Research Building Blocks of Reading Instruction: Kindergarten to Grade 3*. Washington: National Institute for Literacy.

Ausubel, D.P. 1963. *The Psychology of Meaningful Verbal Learning*. New York: Bruner and Stratton.

Babbie, E. and Mouton, J. 2001. *The Practice of Social Research*. Cape Town: Oxford University.

Baker, L. and Brown, A. 1984. Metacognitive Skills and Reading.In D. Pearson (Ed.), *Handbook of Reading Research*. New York: Longman, 355-394.

Bandura, A. 1977. *Social Learning Theory*. Englewood Cliffs: Prentice Hall.

Bandura, A. 1994. *Self-Efficacy: The Exercise of Control*. New York: W.H. Freeman.

Bandura, A. 1994. Self-Efficacy. In V.S. Ramachaudran (Ed.), *Encyclopaedia of Human Behaviour*, 4: 71-78.

Bassey, M. 1999. *Case Study Research in Educational Settings*. Buckingham: Open University.

Beck, I.L. and McKeown, M.G., 2001.Text Talk: Capturing the Benefits of Read Aloud Experiences for Young Children, *Reading Teacher*, 55(1): 10-20.

Beck, I.L., McKeown, M.G., Hamilton, R.L. and Kucan, L. 1997. *Question the Author: An Approach for Enhancing Student Engagement with Text*. New York: International Reading Association.

Ben-Ari, R and Kedem-Friedrich, P. 2000. Restructuring Heterogenous Classes for Cognitive Development Social Interactive Perspective, *Instructional Science*, 28(2), 153-167.

Bender, S.J., Neutens, J.J., Skonie-Hardin, S. and Sorochan, W.D. 1997.*Teaching Health Science, Elementary and Middle School (4th ed)*. Boston: Jones & Bartlett.

Bender, W.N. 2002. *Differentiating Instruction for Students with Learning Disabilities: Best Practices for General and Special Educators*. Thousand Oaks: Corwin.

Berry, G., Hall, D. and Gildroy, P.G. 2004.Teaching Learning Strategies. In B.K. Lenz, D.D. Deshler and B.R. Kissam (Eds.), *Teaching Content for All: Evidence Based Inclusive Practices in Middle and Secondary Schools*. Boston: Pearson Education: 258-278.

Biddulph, J. 2000. Guided Reading in Theoretical Understandings. In Learning Media (Eds.). *Steps to Guided Reading: A Professional Development Course for Grade 3 and Beyond, Course Book.* Huntington Beach: Pacific Learning: 38-46.

Biehler, R.F. and Snowman, J. 1993. *Psychology Applied to Teaching*. Boston: Houghton Mifflin.

Bigge, M.L and Shermis, S.S. 1999. *Learning Theories for Teachers (6th ed).* New York: Longman.

Blachowicz, C. and Ogle, D. 2001. *Reading Comprehension: Strategies for Independent Learners*. New York: Guilford.

Bloch, C. 1999. Literacy in the Early Years: Teaching and Learning in Multilingual Early Childhood Classrooms, *International Journal of Early Years Education*, 7(1):39-51.

Block, C.C. and Pressley, M. 2002. *Comprehension Instruction: Research Based Best Practice*. New York: Guilford.

Block, C.C., Gambrell, L.B. and Pressley, M. (Eds.). 2002. *Improving Comprehension Instruction: Rethinking Research, Theory, and Classroom Practice*. San Francisco: Jossey Bass.

Bloom, B.S. 1968. Learning Mastery, *Evaluation Comment*,1(2): 1-12.

Bos, C.S. and Vaughn, S. 1994. *Strategies for Teaching Students with Learning and Behaviour Problems*. Boston: Allyn and Bacon.

Brand-Gruwel, S., Aarnoutse, C.A.J. and Van den Boss, K.P. 1998. Improving Text Comprehension Strategies in Reading and Listening Setting, *Learning and Instruction*, 8(1):63:81.

Braun, V. and Clarke, V. 2006. Using Thematic Analysis in Psychology, *Qualitative Research in Psychology*, 3:77-101.

Bruner, J. 1986. *Actual Minds: Possible Worlds*. Cambridge: Harvard University.

Bukatko, D. and Daehler, M.W. 2001.*Child Development: A Thematic Approach*. Boston: Houghton Mifflin.

Burke, J. 2000. *Reading Reminders: Tools, Tips and Techniques*. Portmouth: Boynton-Cook.

Burns, M., Griffin,P., and Snow, C. 1999. Starting out right: a guide to promoting children's reading success. In P. Westwood (Ed.), Reading and learning difficulties (p. 5). Camberwell,Victoria: Australian Council for Educational Research.

Burns, M., Griffin, P., and Snow, C. 1999. Starting out right: a guide to promoting children's reading success.Washington, D.C.: National Academy Press.

Westwood, P. 2001. Reading and learning difficulties: Approaches to teaching and assessment. Camberwell, Victoria: ACER.

Lerner, J. 1997. Learning disabilities, theories,diagnosis and teaching strategies (6th ed.), New York: Haughton Miffin.

Butcher, K.R. and Kintsch, W. 2003.Text Comprehension and Discourse Processing. In A.F. Healey and R.W. Proctor and B. Weiner (Eds.),

Handbook of Psychology, Vol.4, Experimental Psychology. New York: Wiley. (pp. 575-595).

Butler. S., Urrutia, K., Buenger, A. and Hunt. M. 2010. *A Review of the Current Research on Comprehension Instruction*. National Reading Technical Assistance Center (NRTAC): RMC Research Corporation.

Cain, K., Oakhill, J. and Bryant, P. 2004. Children's Reading Comprehension Ability: Concurrent Prediction by Working Memory, Verbal Ability, and Component Skills, *Journal of Educational Psychology*, 96:31-42.

Campbell, J.R., Kelly, D.L., Mullis, I.V.S., Martin, M.O. and Sainsbury, M. 2001. *Framework and Specifications for PIRLS Assessment 2001*. Online Available: http://www.iea.nl/iea/hq/index.php?id=96&type=1. Retrieved: 17 March 2009.

Carr, D. 1996. The Dichotomy of Liberal versus Vocational Education: Some Basic Conceptual Geography. In *Philosophy of Education* (1995 ed). Alven Neiman (Urbana III: Philosophy of Education Society, 1996), 53-63.

Carter, V.E. 2000. *New Approaches to Literacy Learning: A Guide for Teacher Educators*. UNESCO, France.

Chaote, J.S. and Rakes, T.A. 2004. Recognizing Words as Tools for Reading Comprehension. In J.S. Chaote(Ed.). *Successful Inclusive Teaching: Proven Ways to Detect and Correct Special Needs*. Boston: Pearson.

Chafin, R., Morris, R.K., &Seely, R.E. 2001. Learning New Word Meanings from Context: A Study of Eye Movements, *Journal of Experimental Psychology: Learning, Memory, and Cognition*, 27: 225-235.

Charmaz, K. 2000. Grounded Theory, Objectives and Constructivist Methods. In: Denzin, N.K. and Lincoln,Y.S. (Eds.). *Handbook of Qualitative Research (2nd ed.)*. London: Sage.

Chia, H.L. 2001. Reading Activities for Effective Top-Down Processing, *Forum*, 39(1):22.

Christ, T. and Wang, X.C. 2010. Bridging the Vocabulary Gap: What the Research Tells us about Vocabulary Instruction in Early Childhood, *Research in Review*. Online Available: www.naeyc.org. Retrieved: 27 June 2012.

Christen, W.L. and Murphy, T.J. 1991. Increasing Comprehension by Activating Prior Knowledge. ERIC Digest. Bloomington: In *ERIC Clearinghouse on Reading, English, and Communication*. [ED 328 885].

Clark, K.F. 2004. What can I say besides 'Sounding it out'? Coaching Word Recognition in Beginning Reading, *International Reading Association*, 57(5): 440-449.

Clay, M.M. 1993. An Observation Survey of Early Literacy Achievement. Auckland: Heinemann.

Cohen, D.K. 1996. Standards-Based School Reform: Policy, Practice and Performance. In Ladd, H. (Ed.). *Holding Schools Accountable: Performance-Based Reform in Education*. Washington: The Brookings Institution.

Cohen, L., Manion. L., and Morrison, K. 2000. *Research Method in Education*. London: Routledge Falmer.

Cohen, V.L. and Cohen, J.L. 2008.*Literacy for Children in an Information Age: Teaching Reading, Writing and Thinking*. Canada: Thomson Wadsworth.

Cooper, J.D. 2000. *Literacy: Helping Children Construct Meaning* (4th ed.). Boston: Houghton Mifflin.

Cortesse, P. and Middleton, K. 1994.*The Comprehensive School Health Challenge: Promoting through Education*. Santa Cruz: ETR.

Crawford, E.C. and Torgesen, J.K. 2006.*Teaching all Students to Read: Practices from Reading first Schools with Strong Intervention Outcomes*. Tallahassee: Florida Center for Reading Research.

Creswell, J.W. 2008. *Educational Research: Planning, Conducting, and Evaluating Quantitative and Qualitative Research.* (3rd ed.). Upper Saddle Creek. Pearson Education.

Criticos, C., Long, L., Moletsane, R. and Mthiyane, N. 2002. Getting Practical: About Outcomes-based Teaching. Learning Guide. *South African Institute for Distance Education and Oxford University Press*. Cape Town: Oxford University.

Cummins, J. 1992. Language Proficiency, Bilingualism, and Academic Achievement. In P.A. Richard-Amato and M.A. Snow (Eds.). *The Multicultural Classroom*. New York: Longman: 91-104.

Cunningham, P.M. and Allington, R.L. 1999.*Classrooms that Work*. New York: Addison-Wesley.

D'Ambrosio, M. 2004. *Asking Questions as you Read*. Online Available: www./ edu/masters_in_teaching.Retrieved: 14 June 2011.

Denzin, N.K. and Lincoln, Y.S. (Eds.). 1994. *Handbook of Qualitative Research*. Thousand Oaks: Sage.

Denzin, N.K. and Lincoln, Y.S. (Eds.). 2000. *Handbook of Qualitative Research (2^{nd}ed)*. London: Sage.

De Vos, A.S. 1998. *Research at Grassroots: A Primer for the Caring Profession*. Pretoria: Van Schaik.

Department of Education (DoE). 1997. *Curriculum 2005 (C2005). Lifelong Learning for the 21^{st}Century*. Pretoria: Department of Education.

Department of Education (DoE), 2002. *Revised National Curriculum Statement Grades R-9 (Schools). Languages: English-Home Language*. Pretoria: Department of Education.

Department of Education (DoE), 2003. *Revised National Curriculum Statement Grade R-9 (Schools). Teacher's Guide for the Development of Learning Programmes. Foundation Phase*. Pretoria: Department of Education.

Department of Education (DoE), 2008. Foundations for Learning. *Government Gazette*, Pretoria: Department of Education.

Department of Education (DoE), 2008. *National Reading Strategy*. Pretoria: Department of Education.

Department of Education (DoE), 2008. *Teaching Reading in the Early Grades: Teacher's Handbook*. Pretoria: Department of Education.

Department of Basic Education (DBE). 2010. *Curriculum and Assessment Policy Statement (CAPS)*. Pretoria: DBE.

Dewitz, P. 2006. Reading Comprehension in Five Basal Reading Programs. *Paper Presented at the Annual Meeting of the National Reading Conference*, Los Angeles.

Dole, J.A. 2000. Comprehension Strategies. Literacy in America: An Encyclopedia of History, *Theory and Practice*.1: 85-88.

Dole, J.A., Duffy, G.G., Roehler, L. and Pearson, P.D. 1999. Moving from the Old to the New: Research on Reading Comprehension Instruction, *Review of Educational Research*, 61:239-264.

Dreyer, C. 1998. Improving Students' Reading Comprehension by Means Strategy Instruction, *Journal of Language Teaching*, 32:18-29.

Driscoll, M.P. 1994. *Psychology of Learning for Instruction*. Needham Heights: Allyn and Bacon.

Droop, N. and Verhoeven, L. 1998. Background Knowledge, Linguistic Complexity and Second Language Reading Comprehension, *Journal of Literacy Research*, 30(2): 253-271.

Du Plessis, S. 2006. *Multilingual Preschool Learners: A Collaborative Approach to Communication Intervention, Doctoral Thesis*. Pretoria: University of Pretoria.

Duffy, G. 2003. *Explaining Reading: A Resource for Teaching Concepts, Skills, and Strategies*. New York: Guilford.

Duffy, G.G. and Mclntyre, L.D. 1982. A Naturalistic Study of Instructional Assistance in Primary-Grade Reading, *Elementary School Journal*, 83: 15-23.

Duffy, G.G. 2002.The Case for Direct Explanation of Strategies. In C.C. Block and M. Pressley (Eds.), *Comprehension Instruction: Research-based Best Practices*. New York:Wiley, 28-41.

Duke, N.K. and Pearson, P.D. 2002. Effective Practices for Developing Reading comprehension. In A.E. Farstup and S.J. Samuels (Eds.).*What Research has to Say about Reading Instruction (3rd ed.)*. New Work: International Reading Association, 205-242.

Duke, N.K. and Pearson, P.D. 1992. Effective Practices for Developing Reading Comprehension. In A.E. Farstrup and S.J. Samuels (Eds.).*What Research has to Say about Reading Instruction*. New Work: International Reading Association, 40-65.

Duke, N.K. and Pearson, P.D. 2002. Effective Practices for Developing Reading Comprehension. *From what Research has to Say about Reading Instruction.*

Scholastic Red. Professional Article (3rd ed.). DE: International Reading Association, 205-242.

Duke, N.K. 2003. Reading to Learn from the very Beginning: Information Books in Early Childhood, *Young Children*, 58(2):14-20.

Durkin, D. 1978. What Classroom Observations Reveal about Reading Comprehension, *Reading Research Quarterly*, 16:515-544.

Durkin, D. 1979. What Classroom Observations Reveal about Reading Comprehension Instruction, *Reading Research Quarterly*, 14(4): 481-533.

Durkin, D. 1981. Reading Comprehension Instruction in Five Basal Reading Series, *Reading Research Quarterly*, 16(4): 514-544.

Durkin, D. 1990. Matching Classroom Instructions with Reading Abilities: An Unmet Need, *Remedial and Special Education*, 11 (3): 23-28.

Durkin, D.1993. *Teaching them to Read (6th ed.)*. Needham: Allyn and Bacon.

Eggen, P. and Kauchak, D. 2001.*Windows in the Classrooms*. New Prentice Hall.

Ehren, B.J. 2005. Responsiveness to Intervention and the Speech-Language Pathologist, *Topics in Language Disorders, 25*(2): 310-321.

Ehri, L.C. and Sweet, J. 1991. Fingerpoint-Reading: Is the First Stage of Printed Word Learning Visual or Phonetic? *Reading Research Quartely*, 20: 163-179.

Engelbrecht, P. and Green, L. 2001. *Promoting Learner Development: Preventing and Working with Barriers to Learning*. Pretoria: Van Schaik.

Engler, B. 1985. *Personalities Theories: An Introduction (2nd ed.)*. Boston: Houghton Mifflin.

Ephraim, K. 2009. *Reading Comprehension Instruction for Oxpository Text in Elementary Education*. Liberty University (Senior Thesis).

Evans, R. 2005. *Explaining Low Leaner Participation during Interactive Television Instruction in a Developing Country Context*. Pretoria: University of Pretoria (PhD Thesis).

Farrell, T.S.C. 2001. Teaching reading Strategies: 'It Takes Time!'*Reading in a Foreign Language,* 13(2), 631-646.

Fawson, P.C. and Reutzel, R.D. 2000. But I only have a Basal: Implementing Guided Reading in the Early Grades, *Reading Teacher,* 54(1): 84-98.

Fielding, L. and Pearson, D. 1994. Reading Comprehension: What Works, *Educational Leadership*, 5:62-66.

Fisher, D., Frey, N. and Williams, D. 2002.Seven Literacy Strategies that Work, *Educational Leadership*, 60 (3):70-73.

Fisher, R. 1998. Thinking about Thinking: Developing Metacognition in Children, *Early Child Development and Care*, 141: 1-15.

Flavell, J.H.1976. Metacognitive Aspects of Problem Solving. In L.B. Resnick (Ed.), *The Nature of Intelligence.* Hillsdale: Erlbaum.

Fleisch, B. 2008. *Primary Education in Crisis: Why South African School Children Underachieve in Reading and Mathematics*. South Africa: Shumani.

Flynt, E.S. and Cooter, R.B. (Jr). 2005. Improving Middle-Grades Reading in Urban Schools: The Memphis Comprehension Framework.Issues in Urban Literacy,*The Reading Teacher*, 58(8).

Fountas, I. and Pinnell, G. 2001. *Guiding Readers and Writers: Grades 3-6 Teaching Comprehension, Genre and Content Literacy*. Portsmouth: Heinemann.

Fountas, I. 1996. *Guided Reading. Good First Teaching for all Children*. Portsmouth: Heinemann.

Fraser, W. 1990. *Didactics for the Undergraduate Student (2nd ed)*. Durban: Butterworth.

Freedman, J. and Combs, G. 1996. *Narrative Therapy. The Social Construction of Preferred Realities*. New York: W.W. Norton.

Gage, N.L. and Berliner, D.C. 1992. *Educational Psychology*. Boston: Houghton Mifflin.

Garcia, T. &Pintrich, P.R. 1994. Regulating Motivation and Cognition in the Classroom: The Role of Self-Schemas and Self-Regulatory Strategies. In D.H. Schunk and B.J. Zimmerman (Eds.). *Self-regulation of Learning and Performance: Issues and Educational Applications*. Hillsdale: Lawrence Erlbaum, 127-153.

Gardiner, S. 2005. *Building Student Literacy through Sustained Silent Reading*. Alexandria: Association for Supervision Curriculum Development.

Gay, L.R. 1996. Educational Research.Competencies for Analysis and Application. Englewood: Merrill.

Gersten, R., Fuchs, L.S., Williams, J.P., and Baker, S. 2001. Teaching Reading Comprehension Strategies to Students with Learning Disabilities: A Review of Research, *Review of Educational Research,* 71(2), 279-320.

Gibson, A. 2004. Reading for Meaning: Tutoring Elementary Students to Enhance Comprehension, *TutorNewsletter*. Online Available: www.readingrockets. org/article/22800. Retrieved: 12 November 2011.

Goldenberg, H. and Goldenberg, I. 2008. *Family Therapy.An Overview*. Belmont: Thomson Brooks/Cole.

Graves, M., Juel, C. and Graves, B. 2001. *Teaching Reading in the 21st Century (3rd ed.)*. Boston: Allyn and Bacon.

Graves, M.F. 2006. *The Vocabulary Book: Learning and Instruction*. New York: Teachers College.

Green, J.F. 1999. *Morphemes for Meaning*. Longmont: Spris West.

Guastello, E.F. and Lenz, C. 2005. Student Accountability: Guided Reading Kid Stations,*Reading Teacher,* 59(2): 144-156.

Guthrie, J.T. and Davis, M.H. 2003. Motivating Struggling Readers in Middle School through an Engagement Model of Classroom Practice, *Reading and Writing Quarterly*, 19: 5985.

Guthrie, J.T. and Wingfield, A. 2000. Engagement and Motivation in Reading. In M.L. Kamil, P.B. Mosenthal, P.D. Pearson, and R. Barr (Eds.). *Handbook of Reading Research, Vol.3*. Mahwah: Erlbaum, 403-422.

Haas, G. and Parkay, F.W. 1993. *Curriculum Planning: A New Approach (6thed)*. Boston: Allyn and Bacon.

Hall, K.J. and Walsh, M. 2002.Teacher Student Interaction and Language Learning, *Annual Review of Applied Linguistics*, 22, 186-203.

Harris, T.L. and Hodges, R.E. 1995. *The Literacy Dictionary: The Vocabulary of Reading and Writing*. New York: International Reading Association.

Harvey, S. and Goudvis, A. 2007. *Strategies that Work: Teaching Reading Comprehension for Understanding and Engagement (2nded)*. Portland: Sternhouse.

Hattie, J.A. 2003. Teachers Make a Difference: What is the Research Evidence? *Background Paper to Invited Address Presented at the 2003 ACER Research Conference*. Carlton Crest Hotel, Melbourne, Australia, October 19-2, 2003. Online Available:http://www.acer.edu.au/workshops/documents/Teachers Makea Difference hattie.pdf.Retrieved: 10 September 2011.

Heidin, L.R. and Conderman,G. 2010. Teaching Students to Comprehend Information Text through Re-reading, *The Reading Teacher*, 63(7): 556-565.

Hjelle, L.A. and Ziegler,D.J.1981. *Personality Theories Basis Assumptions, Research and Application*. Auckland: McGraw Hill.

Henk, W.A., Moore, J.C., Marinak, B.A. and Tomasetti, B. 2000. A Reading Lesson Observation Framework for Elementary Teachers, Principals, and Literacy Supervisors, *The Reading Teacher*, 53(5): 358-369.

Heugh, K. 2005. A History of Mother-Tongue and Bilingual Education in South Africa.In S.B. Neuman and D.K. Dickinson (Eds.). *Handbook of Early Literacy Research*. New York: Guilford, 211-231.

Hodge, C. 2009. Reading Comprehension for Elementary Classrooms. Online Available: www.helium.com. Retrieved: 14 April 2008.

Hoffman, L.1990. Constructing Realities: An Art of Lenses, *Family Process*, 29(1), 1-12.

Hornsby, D. 2000. *A Closer Look at Guided Reading. Armadale Vic Eleanor Curtain*. Online Available:http://www.societyforqualityeducation.org/newsletter/1651-wordly.pdf.Retrieved: 18 June 2009.

Hopkins, D. 1996. *A Teaching Guide to Classroom Research*. Buckingham: Open University.

Howie, S.J., Venter, E., Van Staden, S., Zimmerman, L., Long, C., Scherman, V. and Archer, E. 2007. *PIRLS 2006 Summary Report: South African Children's*

Reading Achievement. Pretoria: University of Pretoria, Centre for Evaluation and Assessment.

Howie, S.J. 2006. Multi-Level Factors Affecting the Achievement of South African Pupils in Mathematics. In Howie, S.J. and Plomp, T. (eds). *Contexts of Learning and Science*. Oxon: Routledge.

Ivy, G. and Fisher, D. 2005. Learning from what Doesn't Work, *Educational Leadership*, 63(2): 8-40.

Jackson, G. 2003. *A Comparative Case Study of the Strategies used by Grade 1 Teachers who Teach through the Medium of English*. Rhodes University, Grahamstown (Unpublished Master's Thesis).

Jamieson, D.G. 2009. National Strategy for Early Literacy: Summary Report. *The Canadian Language and Literacy Research Network*.Online Available: http://docs.cllrnet.ca/NSEL/finalReport.pdf.Retrieved: 26 July 2011.

Jansen, J. 2005. *Educationally Essential: Teachers, Textbooks and Time. Conflict and Governance: Transformation Audit*. Cape Town: Institute for Justice and Reconciliation.

Jansen, J.D. 2002. *Mergers in High Education: Theorising Change in Transitional Context. Lessons Learnt in Transitional Context*. Pretoria: Unisa.

Janzen, J.E. 2003.*Understanding the Nature of Autism: A Guide to the Autism Spectrum Disorders (2nd ed.)*. San Antonio: Therapy Skill Builders.

JET Education Services. 2010. *Foundation Phase Literacy and the Gaps in the System: A Report Prepared by Room to Read*. Johannesburg: JET.

Joubert, I., Bester, M., & Meyer, E. 2008. Literacy in the Foundation Phase. Pretoria. Van Schaick Publishers.

Joshua, J. 2001. *Foundation Phase: Literacy-Module 1. Learning Guide: National Professional Diploma in Education (NPDE)*. Durban: University of Natal.

Kail, R.V. 2001. *Children and their Development (2nded)*. Upper Saddle River: Prentice-Hall.

Kamper, G., Schulze, S. and Goodwin-Davey, A. 1999. Action Research. In G. Kamper and A. Goodwin-Davey(Eds.). *Journey from Theory to Practice*. Pretoria: University of South Africa.

Kauchak, D.P. and Eggen, P.D. 1998. *Learning and Teaching: Research Based Methods (3rded.)*. Boston: Allyn and Bacon.

Keen, E.O. 2002. From Good to Memorable: Characteristics of Highly Effective Comprehension Teaching. In C.C. Block, L.B. Gambrell, and C.M. Pressley (Eds.). *Improving Comprehension Instruction. Rethinking Research, Theory and Classroom Practice*. San Francisco: Jossey-Bass, 80-105.

Keene, E. and Zimmerman, S. 1997. *Mosaic of Thought*. Portsmouth: Heinemann.

Kilfoil, W.R. and Van der Walt, C. 1997. *Learn to Teach. English Language Teaching in a Multilingual Context*. Pretoria: Van Schaik.

Kirby, J.R. 2007. Reading Comprehension: Its Nature and Development. *Encyclopaedia of Language and Literacy Development*. London: Canadian Language and Literacy Research Network. Online Available: http://www.literacyencyclopedia.ca/pdfs/topic.php?top[d=227. Retrieved: 12 June 2009.

Klinger, J.K. and Vaughn, S.1999. Promoting Reading Comprehension, Content Learning and English Acquisition through Collaborative Strategic Reading (CSR), *The Reading Teacher*, 52(7): 738-747.

Klingner, J.K., Vaughn, S. and Boardman, A. 2007. *Teaching Reading Comprehension to Students with Learning Difficulties*. New York: Guilford.

Kolic-Vehovec, S. 2006. Metacognitive Strategies and Reading Comprehension in Elementary School Students, *European Journal of Psychology of Education*. xx1(4), 439-451.

Krog, A. 2006. *Presentation at the Principals' Evening Meeting*. Cape Town: University of Western Cape.

Kragler, S., Walker, C.A., and Martin, L.E. 2005. Strategy Instruction in Primary Content Textbooks, *The Reading Teacher*, 59(3), 254-261.

Krueger, A.B. 1994. *Focus Groups: A Practical Guide for Applied Research (2nd ed.)*. London: SAGE.

Kruizinga, A. and Nathanson, R. 2010. An Evaluation of Guided Reading in Three Primary Schools in the Western Cape, *Per Linguam: Journal of Language Learning*, 26(2):67-76.

Kruizinga, A. 2010. *An Evaluation of Guided Reading in Three Primary Schools in the Western Cape*. Stellenbosch: University of Stellenbosch (Master's Thesis).

Kosanovich, M., Ladinsky, K., Nelson, L. and Torgesen, J. 2006. *Differentiated Reading Instruction: Small Group Lesson Structures for all Students*. Tallahassee: Florida Center for Reading Research.

Kvale, S. and Brinkmann, S. 2009. *Interviews: Learning the Craft of Qualitative Research Interviewing (2nd ed)*. Thousand Oaks: SAGE.

Lane, H.B. and Wright, T.L. 2007. Maximizing the Effectiveness of Reading Aloud, *The Reading Teacher*, 60 (7): 668-675.

Langer, E.J. 1997. *The Power of Mindful Learning*. Reading: Merloyd Lawrence.

Langer, J.A. 1984. Examining Background Knowledge and Text Comprehension, *Reading Quartely*, 4:468-481.

Langer, D.L. 1997. Comprehension Strategies Instruction: Does it Made a Difference? *Reading Psychologist*, 18(G):31-68.

Learning First Alliance, 1998. *Every Child Reading: An Action Plan of the Learning First Alliance*. Washington: The National Research Council (NRC).

Lehr, F. and Osborn, J. 2005. *Focus on Reading Comprehension.*Online Available: www.prel.org/programs/rel/rel.asp. Retrieved: 12 November 2011.

Lehr, F., Osborn, J. and Hiebert, E.H. 2004. *Focus on Vocabulary*. Honolulu: Pacific Regional Educational Laboratory.

Lehr, F. and Osborn, J. 2006. *Focus on Comprehension*. Honolulu: Pacific Regional Educational Laboratory.

Lenz, K. 2005. An Introduction to Reading Comprehension. Online Available: http://www.Special connections.ku.edu.Retrieved: 12 March 2009.

Lessing, A.C. and De Witt, M.W. 2005.*Teaching Reading in an OBE Framework.* Pretoria: University of South Africa.

Lieberman, L.D., Clark, N.M., Krone, K.V., Orlandi, M.A. and Wynder, E.L. 1992.The Relationship between Cognitive Maturity and Information about Health Problems among School Age Children, *Health Education Research*: 391-401.

Long, C. and Zimmerman, L. 2008. *Reading beyond the Lines: Developing South African Foundation Phase Learners' High Order Reading Literacy Skills*. Online Available: http://www.cepd.org.za/files/CEPD-TEP-conf2008-LongZimmerman.paf. Retrieved: 24 February 2009.

Loranger, A.L. 1997. Comprehension Strategies Instruction: Does it Make a Difference? Reading Psychology. 18(10), 31-68.

Louw, D.A.1991. *Human Development*. Pretoria: Haum Tertiary.

Lubliner, S., and Smetana, L. 2005. The Effects of Comprehensive Vocabulary Instruction on Title 1 Students' Metacognitive Word-Learning Skills and Reading Comprehension, *Journal of Literacy Research*, 37(2): 163-200.

Luckett, K.1992. *National Additive Bilingualism. Report from the Medium of Instruction Sub-group to the Language Policy Research Group (NEPI).*South Africa: Working Paper.

Lyon, C. 2003. *Teaching Struggling Readers*. Portsmouth: Heinemann.

Lyon, G.R., Shaywitz, S.F., and Shaywitz, B.A. 2003. Defining Dyslexia, Comorbidity, Teachers' Knowledge of Language Reading, *Annals of Dyslexia*, 53: 1-14.

Lysynchuk, L.M. and Vye, N.J. 1990. Reciprocal Teaching Improves Standardized Reading-comprehension Performance in Poor Comprehenders, *Elementary School Journal*, 90(5): 469-484.

MacMillan, J.H. and Schumacher, S. 2001. *Research in Education: A Conceptual Introduction (5th ed)*. New York: Harper Collins.

Mankveld, H. and Pepler, A. 2004. *Geletterheidsontwikkeling by Graad R-Leerders: 'n Gevalle Studie*, Per Linguam: Journal of Language Learning, 20(2): 46-61.

Maree, K. 2011. *First Steps in Research*. Van Schaik Publishers: Pretoria.

Maria, K.1990. *Reading Comprehension Instruction: Issues and Strategies*. Parkton: York.

Marzano, R.J., Pickering, D.J. and Pollack, J.E. 2001. *Classroom Instruction that Works: Research-based Strategies for Increasing Student Achievement*. Columbus: Pearson.

Masters, G.N. and Forster, M. 1997. *Assessment and Reporting. Monitoring Learning. Australia Council for Educational Research. Literacy Standards in Australia*.Online Available:www.http://research.acer.edu.au. Retrieved: 21January 2010.

Mastropieri, M.A., Scruggs, T.E. and Graetz, J.E. 2003. Reading Comprehension Instruction for Secondary Students: Challenges for Struggling Students and Teachers, *Learning Disability Quarterly*, 26(2):103-116.

Maxwell, J.A. 2005. *Qualitative Research Design: An Interactive Approach (2nd ed.)*. Thousand Oaks: Sage.

May, T. 2002. *Qualitative Research in Action*. London: Sage.

Mayer, R. 2003. Learning and Instruction.Upper Saddle River: Pearson Education.

Maykut, P. and Morehouse, R. 1994. *Beginning Qualitative Research: A Philosophical and Practical Guide*. London: The Falmer.

Mazzoni, G. and Cornoldi, C. 1993. Strategies in Study Time Allocation: Why is Study Time Sometimes not Effective? *Journal of Experimental Psychology*, 122: 47-60.

McDavitt, D.S. 1993. *Teaching for Understanding: Attaining Higher Order Learning and Increased Achievement through Experiential Instruction*.ERIC Document Reproduction Service No. ED 374 093.

McEwan, E.K. 2004. *7 Strategies of Highly Effective Readers*. California: Corwin.

MCGregor, T. 2007. *Comprehension Connections: Bridges to Strategic Reading*. Portsmouth: Heinemann.

McKeown M.G. and Beck, I.L. 2004.Direct and Rich Vocabulary. In J.F. Baumann and E.J. Kame'enui (Eds.). *Vocabulary Instruction*. New York. Guilford, 13-27.

McLaughlin, M. and Allen, M.B. 2002. *Guided Comprehension: A Teaching Model for Grades 3-8*. New York: International Reading Association.

McMahon, M. and Oliver, R. 2003. Self-Regulated Learning. In C. McNaught and D. Lassner (Eds.). *Proceedings of Ed-Media 2003*. 2464-2470.

McMaster, K.L., Fuchs, L. and Fuchs, L.S. 2006. Research on Peer-assisted Learning Strategies: The Promise and Limitations of Peer-mediated Instruction, *Reading and Writing Quarterly*, 22: 5-25.

McMillan, J.H. and Schumacher, S. 2001. *Research in Education: A Conceptual Introduction*. London: Longman.

McNeil, J.D. 1992. *Reading Comprehension. New Directions for Classroom Practice (3rd ed)*. New York: Harper Collins.

McPherson, K. 2007. Teacher-Librarians as Reading Guides, *Reading Teacher*, 35(2): 70-73.

Merriam, S.B. 1998. *Qualitative Research in Practice. Examples for Discussion and Analysis*.San Francisco: Jossey-Bass.

Merriam, S.B. 2002. *Qualitative Research in Practice. Examples for Discussion and Analysis*. San Francisco: Jossey-Bass.

Mertens, D. 1998. *Research and Evaluation in Education Psychology. Integrating Diversity with Quantitative, Qualitative, and Mixed Methods (2nd ed.)*. London: Sage.

Messick, S. 1995. Standards of Validity and the Validity of Standards in Performance Assessment, *Educational Measurement: Issues and Practices*, 14(4): 5-8.

Miller, D. 2002. *Reading with Meaning: Teaching Comprehension in the Primary Grades*. Portland: Stenhouse.

Moats, L, 2002. *Professional Development*. Speech Presented at The Secretary's Reading Leadership Academy. Washington DC.

Mokhtari, K. and Reichard, C.A. 2002. Assessing Students' Metacognitive Awareness of Reading Strategies, *Journal of Educational Psychology*, 94(2): 249-259.

Mooney, C.G. 2000. *Theories of Childhood: An Introduction to Dewey, Montesori, Erickson, Piaget* and *Vygotsky*. St. Paul: Redleaf.

Morgan, L. and Goldstein, H. 2004. Teaching Mothers of Low Socio-economic Status to use Decontextualised Language during Story Book Reading, *Journal of Early Intervention*, 26:235-252.

Moswane, A.P. 2002. *Parental Involvement in the Learning of English Second Language among Sepedi-Speaking Communities*. University of the North (Limpopo) (Master's Thesis).

Mothata, J.M., Squelch, J.M., Van der Bank, A.J. and Visser, P.J. 1997. *Understanding the Schools Act*. Pretoria:Department of Education.

Mouton, J.1996.*Understanding Social Research*. Pretoria: Van Schaik.

Mouton, J. 2001. *How to Succeed in Your Masters* and *Doctoral Studies. A South African Guide and Resource Book*. Pretoria: Van Schaik.

Mullis, I., Martin, M., Gonzalez, E. and Kennedy, A. 2003. *PIRLS 2001. International Report: IEA's Study of Reading Literacy Achievement in Primary Schools in 35 Countries*. Chestnut Hill: Boston College.

Mullis, I.V.S., Kennedy, A.M., Martin, M.O. and Sainsbury, M. 2004. *PIRLS 2006. Assessment Framework and Specifications*. Boston: TIMSS and PIRLS International Study Center.

Mugo, F.W. 2006. Sampling in Research. Online Available: http://www.socialresearchmethods.net/tutorial/mugo/tutorial.htm. Retrieved:12 March 2010.

Mwamwenda, T.S. 2004. *Educational Psychology: An African Perspective. (3rd ed.)*. Isando: Heinemann.

Myers, P.A. 2005. The Princess Storyteller, Clara Clarifier, Quincy Questioner, and the wizard: Reciprocal Teaching Adapted for Kindergarten Students, *The Reading Teacher*, 59(4): 314-324.

Naidoo, I. 2001. *Education Decentralisation in Sub-Saharan Africa. A Review of the Literature* (Unpublished Qualifying Paper for the Harvard Graduates School of Education).

Namibia, Ministry of Education (MEC). 1993. *Toward Education for all: A Development Brief.* Windhoek: Gamsberg MacMillan.

National Association for the Education of Young Children (NAEYC). 1998. Goals for Third Grade: Independent and Productive Reading and Writing (NAEYC). In *Learning to Read and Write: Developmentally Appropriate Practices for Young Children, Part 4: Continuum of Children's Development in Early reading and writing. A joint position of the International reading Association (IRA) and the National Association for the Education of Young Children (NAEYC)*. Online Available: www.adlit.org/article/41/. Retrieved: 24 May 2011.

National Institute of Child Health and Human Development (NICHHD). 2000. *What Works in Comprehension Instruction*. Online Available: www.readingrockets.org/article. Retrieved: 12 November 2011.

National Reading Panel (NRP). 2000. *Teaching Children to Read: An Evidence-based Assessment of the Scientific Research Literature on Reading and its Implications for Reading Instruction*. Washington: National Institute of Child Health and Human Development.

National Research Council, 1998. *Eager to Learn: Educating our Preschoolers*. Washington: National Academy.

Nel, C., Dreyer, C. and Kopper, M. 2004.An Analysis of the Reading Profiles of First- Year Students at Potchefstroom University: A Cross Sectional Study and a Case Study, *South African Journal of Education*, 24(1): 95-103.

Noles, J.D. and Dole, J.A. 2004. Helping Adolescent Readers through Explicit Strategy Instruction. In T.L. Jetton and J.A. Dole (Eds.). *Adolescent Literacy Research and Practice*. New York: Guilford, 162-182.

Norris, S.P. and Phillips, L.M. Reading as Inquiry. In R. Duschl and R. Grandy (Eds.). E*stablishing a Consensus Agenda for K-12 Science Inquiry*. Rotterdam: Sense.

O'Malley, C. and Chamot, A.U. 1990. *Learning Strategies in Second Language Acquisition*. Cambridge: Cambridge University.

Oczkus, L. 2004. *Super 6 Comprehension Strategies*. Norwood: Christopher Gordon.

Opie, C. 2004. *Doing Educational Research. A Guide to First Time Researchers*. London: Sage.

Opitz, M. and Ford, M. 2001. *Reaching Readers: Flexible and Innovative Strategies for Guided Reading*. Portsmouth: Heinemann.

Palincsar, A.S. and Brown, A.L. 1984. Reciprocal Teaching in Comprehension Fostering and Monitoring Activities, *Cognition and Instruction*, 1(2): 117-175.

Palincsar, A.S. and Brown, A.L. 1989. Instruction for Self-regulated Reading. In L.B. Resnick and L.E. Klopfer (Eds.).*Toward the Thinking Curriculum: Current Cognitive Research*. Alexandria: Association for Supervision and Curriculum Development. Yearbook,19-39.

Pardo, L.S. 2004. What Every Teacher Needs to Know about Comprehension, *The Reading Teacher*. 58(3): 274-279.

Paris, H.A. and Paris, S.G. 2007.Teaching Narrative Comprehension Strategies to First Graders,*Cognition and Instruction*, 25(1): 1-44.

Paris, S.G. and Stahl, S.A. 2005.*Children's Reading Comprehension and Assessment*. Mahwah: Lawrence Erlbaum.

Paris, S.G. 2002. When is Metacognition Formative, Debilitating, or Beginning? In P. Chambres, M. Izaute and P.J. Marescеaux (Eds.). *Metacognition: Process, Function and Use*. Dordrecht: Kluwer Academic, 105-120.

Parkey, M. and Hurry, J. Teachers' Use of Questioning and Modelling Comprehension Skills in Primary Classrooms, *Educational Review*, 59(3):299-314.

Patton, M.G. 1990. *Qualitative Education and Research Methods*. Newbury Park: SAGE.

Pearson, P.D. and Gallagher, M.C. 1983. The Instruction of Reading Comprehension, *Contemporary Educational Psychology,* 8: 317-344.

Pearson, P.D. and Raphael, T. 1990. Reading Comprehension as a Dimension of Thinking. In B.F. Jones and L.I. Idol (Eds.). *Dimensions of Thinking and Cognitive Instruction: Implications for Reform, Vol.I*. Hillsdale: Erlbaum, 209-240.

Pearson, P.D.1985. Changing the Face of Reading Comprehension Instruction, *The Reading Teacher*, 38(8):724-738.

Pearson, P.D. 2001. Life in the Radical Middle: A Personal Apology for a Balanced View of Reading. In R. Flippo (Ed.). *Reading Researchers in Search of Common Ground*.Newark: International Reading Association, 78-83.

Pearson, P. and Duke, N. 2002.Comprehension Instruction in the Primary Grades. In C. Block and M. Pressely (Eds.). *Comprehension Instruction: Research-based Best Practices*. New York: The Guilford, 247-258.

Pearson, P.D., Roehler, L.R., Dole, J.A. and Duffy, G.G. 1992. Developing Expertise in Reading Comprehension. In A.E. Farstrup and S.J., Samuels

(Eds.). *What Research has to Say about Reading Instruction (2nd ed)*. New York: International Reading Association, 145-199.

Pereira-Laird, J.A. and Deane,F.P. 1997. Development and Validation of a Self-report Measure of Reading Strategy use, *Reading Psychology*, 18(3): 185-235.

Phillips, L.M., Norris, S.P. and Vavra, K.L. 2007. Reading Comprehension Instruction, *Encyclopedia of Language and Literacy Development*. London: Canadian.

Piaget, J. 1950. *The Psychology of Intelligence*.London: Routledge and Kegan Paul.

Piaget, J.1953. *The Origin of Intelligence in the Child*. London: Routledge and Kegan Paul.

Piaget, J. 1967. *Six Psychological Studies*.New York: Random House.

Piaget, J. 1968. *On the Development of Memory and Identity*. Worcester: Clark.

Pintrich, P.R. 1995. Understanding Self-regulated Learning. In R.J. Menges, and M.D. Svinicki (Eds.). *New Directions for Teaching and Learning Vol. 63*. San Fransisco: Jossey-Bass, iii-12.

Pintrich, P.R., Smith, D., Garcia,T. and Mckeachie,W. 1993. Predictive Validity and Reliability of the Motivated Strategies for Learning Questionnaire (MSLQ), *Educational and Psychological Measurement*, 53: 801-813.

Pollock, M.B and Middleton, K. 1994. *School Health Instruction. Elementary and Middle School Years*.Online Available:www.longwood.edu/assets/cehs/HLTH-465-SYLLABUS-f11.doc.Retrieved: 23 October 2011.

Pressley, M.1998. Comprehension Strategies Instruction. In J. Osborn and F. Lehr (Eds.). *Literacy for all: Issues in Teaching and Learning*. New York: Guilford, 113-133.

Pressley, M. 2002. *Reading Instruction that Works: The Case for Balanced Teaching (2nd ed.)*. New York: Guilford.

Pressley, M. and Afflerbach, P. 1995. *Verbal Protocols of Reading: The Nature of Constructively Responsive Reading*. Hillsdale: Erlbaum.

Pressley, M. 2000. What should Comprehension Instruction be the Instruction of? In M.L. Kamil, P. Mosenthal, P.D. Pearson. and R. Barr (Eds.). *Handbook of Reading Research, Vol. 3*. Mahwah: Erlbaum, 545-561.

Pressley, M. 2001. *Effective Beginning Reading Instruction. Executive Summary and Paper Commissioned by the National Reading Conference*. Chicago: National Reading Conference.

Pressley, M., Wharton-McDonald, R., Mistretta-Hampson, J.M. and Echevaria, M.1998. *The Nature of Literacy Instruction in Ten Grade-4/5 Classrooms in Upstate New York. Scientific Studies of Reading*.Online Available:www.readingrockets.org/article.Retrieved: 12 May 2011.

Pretorius, E. and Ribbens, R. 2005. Reading in a Disadvantaged High School: Issues of Accomplishments, Assessment and Accountability, *South African Journal of Education*, 25(3):139-147.

Pretorius, E.J. 2000. *Reading Ability and Academic Performance in South Africa: Are We Fiddling while Rome is Burning? Language Matters.* Pretoria: University of South Africa.

Prinsloo, J. &Janks, H. 2002. Critical Literacy in South Africa: Possibilities and Constraints in 2002, *English Teaching: Practice and Critique,* 1(1).

Programme for International Student Assessment (PISA). 2000. Online Available:http://www.oect.org. Retrieved: 14 May 2010.

Programme for International Student Assessment (PISA). 2006. Online Available:http://www.oect.org. Retrieved: 14 May 2010.

Puustinen, M. and Pulkkinen, L. 2001. Models of Self-Regulated Learning: A Review, *Scandinavian Journal of Educational Research*, 45:269-286.

Ramphele, M. 2009. Another Generation Betrayed, *The Times*, January 2009:9 and 18.

RAND Reading Study Group. 2002. *Reading for Understanding: Toward an R & D Program in Reading Comprehension*. Santa Monica: RAND Corporation.

Raphael, T. and Au, K. 2005. QAR: Enhancing Comprehension and Test-taking Across Grades and Content Areas, *The Reading Teacher*, 59(3):206-221.

Raphael, T.E. and Wonnacott, C.A. 1985. Heightening Fourth-Grade Students' Sensitivity to Sources of Information for Answering Comprehension Questions, *Reading Quarterly*, 20: 282-296.

Reeves, C., Heugh, K., Prinsloo, C.H., MacDonald, C., Netshitangani, T., Alidou, H., Diedericks, G. and Herbst, D. 2008. *HSRC 2006-2007. Evaluation of Literacy Teaching in Primary Schools of Limpopo Province*. Research Commissioned by the Limpopo Department of Education (LDoE).

Reutzel, D.R., Smith, J.A. and Fawson, P.C. 2005. An Evaluation of Two Approaches for Teaching Reading Comprehension Strategies in the Primary Years using Science Information Texts, *Early Childhood Research Quarterly*, 20: 276-305.

Republic of South Africa (RSA).1997. *South African Schools Act, No. 84 of 1996*. Pretoria: Government Printers.

Reynolds, R. and Brown, K.J. 2001. *Reading Teacher Empowerment through Knowledge: The Role of Cooperative Masters Programs in Professional Development* (Manuscript under Publication).

Rickford, A.E. 2001.The Effects of Teacher Education on Reading Improvement, *Reading Achievement*, 38: 147-169.

Robb, L. 1996. *Reading Strategies that Work: Teaching Students to become Better Readers*. New York: Scholastic.

Roe, B.D., Smith, S.H., and Burns, P.C. 2005. *Teaching Reading in Today's Elementary Schools (9th ed.)*. Boston: Houghton Mifflin.

Roe, B.D., Stoodt, B.D. and Burns, P.C. 1991. *Secondary School Reading Instruction: The Content Areas (4th ed.)*. Boston: Haughton Mifflin.

Ross, K., Saito, M., Dolata, S., Ikeda, M. and Zuze, L. 2004. *SACMEQ, 2004 Data Archive for the SAQMEC I and SACMEQ II Projects*. Paris: International Institute for Educational Planning UNESCO.

Roth, S.F. and Perfetti, C.A. 1980. A Framework for Reading, Language Comprehension, and Language Disability, *Topics in Language Disorders*, 11: 15-27.

Routman, R.1996. *Literacy at the Cross Roads: Crucial Talk about Reading, Writing, and other Teaching Dilemmas*. Portsmouth: Heinemann.

Routman,R. 2000. *Conversations: Strategies for Teaching, Leaning and Evaluation*. Portsmouth: Heinemann.

Schallert, D.L. and Martin, D.B. 2003. A Psychological Analysis of what Teachers and Students do in the Language Arts Classroom. In J. Flood, D. Lapp, J.R. Squire and J.M. Jensen (Eds.). *Handbook of Research on Teaching English Language Arts*. Mahwah: Erlbaum, 31-45.

Schunk, D.H. and Zimmerman, B.J. 1994. *Self-Regulation of Learning and Performance: Issues and Educational Implications*. Hillsdale: Erlbaum.

Schurink, E.M.1998. Designing Qualitative Research.In A.S. De Vos, (ed.). *Research at Grass Roots. A Primer for the Caring Professions*. Pretoria: Van Schaik.

Scott, J.A. and Nagy, W.E. 1997. Understanding the Definitions of Unfamiliar Words, *Reading Research Quarterly*, 32: 184-200.

Shaffer, D.R. 1996. *Developmental Psychology: Childhood and Adolescence*. California: Brooks/Cole.

Schuum, J.S. 2006. *Reading Assessment and Instruction for All Learners*. New York: Guilford.

Shanahan, T. 2006. *The National Reading Panel Report: Practical Advice for Teachers*. Chicago: Learning Point.

Shanahan, T., Callison, K., Carriere, C., Duke, N.K., Pearson, P.D., Schatschneider, C. and Torgeson, J. 2010. *Improving Reading Comprehension in Kindergarten through 3rd Grade: A Practical Guide*. Washington: National Center of Education Evaluation and Regional Assistance, Institute of Education Sciences, U.S. Department of Education.

Silverman, D. 2005. *Doing Qualitative Research (2nd ed)*. Thousand Oaks: Sage.

Singapore Government. 2007. *Press Release. Singapore's Performance in the Progress in International Reading Literacy Study (PIRLS) 2006*. Online Available: http://www.moe.edu.sg/media/press/2007/pr20071129.htm. Retrieved: 29 August 2009.

Singhal, M. 2001. Reading Proficiency, Reading Strategies, Metacognitive Awareness and L2 Readers, *The Meaning Matrix,* 1(1).

Sipe, L.R. 2008. *Story Time: Young Children's Literacy Understanding in the Classroom*. New York: Teachers College.

Snow, C.E., Burns, M.S. and Griffin, P. 1998. *Preventing Reading Difficulties in Young Children.*Washington: National Academy.

Snowball, D. 2005.*Teaching Comprehension: An Interactive Professional Development Course. (Levels K-2, 3-6, 6-9)*. New York: AUSSIE Interactive.

Sporer, N., Brunstein, J.C. and Kieschke, U. 2009. Improving Students' Reading Comprehension Skills: Effects of Strategy Instruction and Reciprocal Teaching, *Learning and Instruction,* 19: 272-286.

Stahl, K.A.D. 2004. Proof, Practice, and Promise: Comprehension Strategy Instruction in Primary Grades, *The Reading Teacher*, 57: 598-609.

Stake, R.E. 1995. *The Art of Case Study Research*. London: Sage.

Stevens, L.P. 2003. A Critical Analysis. Positions and Programs: How are they Changing the Face of Literacy Instruction, *The Reading Teacher*, 56(7): 662-668.

Swaffer, J., Arens, K. and Byrones, H. 1991. *Reading for Meaning: An Integrated Approach to Language Learning*. Englewood Cliffs: Prentice Hall.

Sweet, A.P and Snow, C.E. 2003. *Rethinking Reading Comprehension*. New York: Guilford.

Swanson, P.N. and De-la-Paz, S. 1998.Teaching Effective Comprehension Strategies to Students with Learning and Reading, *Intervention in School and Clinic*, 33(4):209-128.

Swanson, R.A. and Holton, E.F. III (Eds.) 1997. *Human Resource Development Research Handbook: Linking Research and Practice*. San Francisco:Berett-Koehler.

Sweet, A.P. and Snow, C.E. 2002. Reconceptualizing Comprehension. In C.C. Block, L.B. Gambrell and M. Pressley (Eds.). *Improving Comprehension Instruction: Rethinking Research, Theory, and Classroom Practice*. San Francisco: Jossey-Bass, 17-53.

Taberski, S. 2000. *On Solid Ground: Strategies for Teaching Reading in K-3*. Portsmouth: Heinemann.

Taylor, B.M., Pearson, P.D., Peterson, D. and Rodriguez, M.C. 2002. Looking Inside Classrooms Reflecting on the 'How' as well as the 'What' in Effective Reading Instruction, *The Reading Teacher*, 6(3):270-279.

Taylor, B. M., Pearson, P.D., Clark, K. and Walpole, S. 2000. Effective Schools and Accomplished Teachers: Lessons about Primary-grade Instruction in Low-income Schools, *Elementary School Journal*, 101(2): 121-165.

Teale, W.H. 2003. Read Aloud to Children as a Classroom Instructional Activity: Insights from Research to Practice. In A. Van Kleeck, A. A. Stahl and E.B.

Bauer (Eds.). *On Reading Books to Children Parents and Teachers.* Mahwah: Erlbaun, 109-133.

Texas Education Agency. 2002. *Strategies that Promote Comprehension.* Online Available: http://www.reading rockets.org/article.29202. Retrieved: 12 November 2011.

Texas Reading Initiative. 2002. *Research-Based Content Area Reading Instruction.* 2002 Online Revised Edition.

The Nation's Report Card (NAEP). 2004. *Trends in Academic Progress. Three Decades of Student Performance in Reading and Mathematics.* U.S. Department of Education. Institute of Education Sciences.

The Progress in International Reading Literacy Study (PIRLS). 2006. Online Available:http://nces.ed.gov/survey/pirls/index.asp. Retrieved: 4 March 2009.

The SACMEQ (Project) II Report. 2004. *A Study of the Conditions of Schooling and the Quality of Primary Education in Namibia (SACMEQ). Field Report.* International Institute for Educational Planning–UNESCO.

The SACMEQ. 2004. Ross, K., Saito, M., Dolata, S., Ikeda, M. and Zuze, L. 2004. *Data Archive for the SACMEQI and SACMEQ II Projects.* Paris: International Institute for Educational Planning–UNESCO.

The Star. November 7, 2008.

The Sunday Times. 2000. SA Pupils are the Dunces of Africa. 16 July 2000: 1.

The Times. Monday June 13, 2011.

TheTimes. Wednesday June 29, 2011.

Tobias, S. 1994. Interest, Prior Knowledge and Learning, *Review of Educational Research*, 64(1):37-54.

Tompkins, G.E. 2003. *Literacy for the 21st Century: Teaching Reading and Writing in Pre-Kindergarten through Grade 4.* Upper Saddle River: Merrill Prentice Hall.

Torgesen, J., Hauston, D., Rissman, L. and Kosanovich, M. 2007. *Teaching all Students to Read in Elementary School: A Guide to Principals.* Florida: Florida Center for Reading Research, Florida State University.

Torgesen, J.K., Houston, D.D., Rissman, L.M., Decker, S.M., Roberts, G., Vaughn, S., Wexler, J., Francis, D.J., Rivera, M.O. and Lesaux, N. 2007. *Academic Literacy Instruction for Adolescents: A Guidance Document from the Center on Instruction.* Portsmouth: RMC Research Corporation, Center on Instruction.

Trabasso, T. and Bouchard, E. 2002. Teaching Readers How to Comprehend Text Strategically.In C.C. Block and M. Pressley (Eds.). *Comprehension Instruction: Research Based Best Practices.* USA: Guilford, 179-200.

Tregenza, J. and Lewis, M. 2008. *Beyond Simple Comprehension. Literacy Today.* University of Exeter.

Trogenza, J. and Lewis, P. 2009. *Beyond Simple Comprehension.Literacy Today. Project Report, Case Studies and Resource Booklet.*West Sussex Education Authority.

Turner, J. and Paris, S.G. 1995. How Literacy Tasks Influence Children's Motivation for Literacy, The Reading Teacher, 48:62-773.

Uhry, J.K. 2002. *Beginning Reading: A Balanced Approach to Teaching Literacy During the First Three Years at School.* Australia: Allen and Unwin.

Vacca, R.T. and Vacca,J.L. 2000.Writing Across the Curriculum.In R. Indrisano and J.R. Squiri (Eds.). *Perspective on Writing. Research, Theory, and Practice.* New York: International Reading Association, 214-232.

Van den Broek, P. and Kramer, M. 2000. The Mind in Action: What it means to Comprehend During Reading. In B. M.,Taylor, Graves and P.Van den Broek (Eds.). *Reading for Meaning: Fostering Comprehension in the Middle Grades.* New York: International Reading Association, 1-131.

Van Keer, H. 2004. Fostering Reading Comprehension in Fifth Grade by Explicit Instruction in Reading Strategies and Peer Tutoring, *British Journal in Educational Psychology*, 74:37-70.

Van Staden, S. and Howie, S.J. 2008. *South African Teacher Profiles and Emerging Teacher Factors: The Picture Painted by PIRLS 2006.* Online Available:http://www.cepd.org.za/fles CEPD-TED-Conf 2008-Van Staden Howie.paf. Retrieved: 29 May 2009.

Vasta, R., Haith, M.A. and Miller, S.A. 1995.*Child Psychology: The Modern Science.* New York: John Wiley.

Veenman, M.V.J.,Van Hout-Wolters, B.H.A.M. and Afflerbach, P. 2006. *Metacognition and Learning: Conceptual and Methodological Considerations.* Springer: Science and Business Media.

Verhoeven, L. 2000. Components in Early Second Language Reading and Spelling, *Scientific Studies of Reading*, 4(4): 313-330.

Vero'nica, Z. 2008. Reading Comprehension in National and International Programs of Educational Assessment: Scholarship at National Council for Research in Science and Technology (CONICET), *Orientaciony Sociedad*, 81: 19.

Vygotsky, L.L.1968. Mind in Society. *The Development of Higher Psychological Processes.*Harvard: Harvard University.

Vygotsky, L. 1986. *Thought and Language.* Cambridge: MT.

Walraven, M. and Reitsma, P. 1993. The Effect of Teaching Strategies for Reading Comprehension to Poor Readers and the Possible Surplus Effect of Activating Prior Knowledge, *National Reading Conference Yearbook*, 42: 243-250.

Walsh, M.E. and Murphy, J.A. 2003.*Children, Health and Learning. A Guide to the Issues.* London: Praeger.

Wessels, M. 2010. *Practical Guide to Facilitating Language Learning (3rd ed.)*. Southern Africa: Oxford University.

Westera, J. and Moore, D.W. 1995. Reciprocal Teaching of Reading Comprehension in New Zealand High School, *Psychology in Schools*, 32(3): 225-232.

Westwood, P.S. 2004. *Learning and Learning Difficulties: A Handbook for Teachers. Camberwell, VIC: Australian Council for Education (5th ed.)*. Boston: Allyn and Bacon.

Bandura, A. (1986). Social foundations of thought and action: A social cognitive theory. Englewood Cliffs, NJ: Prentice Hall.

Kopp, C. B. (1982). Antecedents of self-regulation: A developmental perspective. *Developmental Psychology, 18*, 199-214.

Mace, F. C., Belfiore, P. J., and Hutchinson, J. M. (2001). Operant theory and research on self-regulation. In B. J. Zimmerman and D. H. Schunk (Eds.), *Self-regulated learning and academic achievement: Theoretical perspectives* (2nd ed., pp. 39-65). Mahwah, NJ: Erlbaum.

Meece, J. L. (2002). *Child and adolescent development for educators* (2nd ed.). Boston: McGraw-Hill.

Schunk, D. H., and Ertmer, P. A. (2000). Self-regulation and academic learning: Self-efficacy enhancing interventions. In M. Boekaerts, P. R. Pintrich, and M. Zeidner (Eds.), *Handbook of self-regulation* (pp. 631-649). San Diego, CA: Academic Press.

Schunk, D. H., and Swartz, C. W. (1993). Goals and progress feedback: Effects on self-efficacy and writing achievement. *Contemporary Educational Psychology, 18*, 337-354.

Vygotsky, L. (1962). *Thought and language*. Cambridge, MA: MIT Press.

Weinstein, C. E., Husman, J., and Dierking, D. R. (2000). Self-regulation interventions with a focus on learning strategies. In M. Boekaerts, P. R. Pintrich, and M. Zeidner (Eds.), *Handbook of self-regulation* (pp. 727-747). San Diego, CA: Academic Press.

Winne, P. H., and Hadwin, A. F. (1998). Studying as self-regulated learning. In D. J. Hacker, J. Dunlosky, and A. C. Graesser (Eds.), *Metacognition in educational theory and practice* (pp. 277-304). Hillsdale, NJ: Erlbaum.

Zimmerman, B. J. (2000). Attaining self-regulation: A social cognitive perspective. In M. Boekaerts, P. R. Pintrich, & M. Zeidner (Eds.), *Handbook of self-regulation* (pp. 13-39). San Diego, CA: Academic Press.

Zimmerman, B. J. (2001). Theories of self-regulated learning and academic achievement: An overview and analysis. In B. J. Zimmerman and D. H. Schunk (Eds.), *Self-regulated learning and academic achievement: Theoretical perspectives* (2nd ed., pp. 1-37). Mahwah, NJ: Erlbaum.

Zimmerman, B. J., and Kitsantas, A. (1999). Acquiring writing revision skill: Shifting from process to outcome self-regulatory goals. *Journal of Educational Psychology, 91*, 241-250.

Zimmerman, B. J., & Martinez-Pons, M. (1990). Student differences in self-regulated learning: Relating grade, sex, and giftedness to self-efficacy and strategy use. *Journal of Educational Psychology, 82*, 51–59.

Williams, T.L. 2007. Reading the Painting: Exploring Visual Literacy in the Primary Grades, *International Reading Association*, 60(7): 636-642.

Woolfolk, A.E. 1995. *Educational Psychology (6th ed)*. Boston: Prentice-Hall.

Wren, S. 2001. The Cognitive Foundations of Learning to Read: A Framework, *Southwest Educational Development Laboratory*. Online Available: www.sedl.org. Retrieved: 01July 2012.

Yang, A. 2007. Cultivating a Reading Habit: Silent Reading at School, *Asian EFL Journal*, 9: 2.

Yin, R.K. 2003. *Application of Case Study Research (2nd ed.)*. Thousand Oaks: Sage.

Yuill, N. and Oakhill, J. 1991. *Children's Problems in Text Comprehension*. Cambridge: Cambridge University.

Scheepers, R.A. 2008. Reading is Fundamental: The Effect of a Reading Programme on Vocabulary Development in a High Poverty Township School, *Per Linguam*, 2(1):30-44.

Zimmerman, B.J. 1989. *Models of Self-Regulated Learning and Academic Achievement. Self-Regulated Learning and Academic Achievement: Theory, Research, and Practice*. New York: Springler.

Zimmerman B.J. 1990. Self-Regulated Academic Learning and Achievement: The Emergence of a Social Cognitive Perspective, *Educational Psychology Review*, 2:173-201.

Zimmerman, B.J. 1998. Academic Studying and Development of Personal Skill: A Self-regulatory Perspective, *Educational Psychologist*, 33:73-86.

Zimmerman,C.B. 1997. Do Reading and Interactive Vocabulary Instruction Make the Difference? An Empirical Study, *TESOL Quarterly*, 31(1): 121-140.

Zimmerman, S. and Hutchins, C. 2003. *7 Keys to Comprehension*. New York: Random House.

Pintrich, P. R. The role of goal orientation in self regulated learning.

Winne, P.H. 1995. Self regulation is ubiquitous but its forms vary with knowledge. Educational Psychologist, 30(4) 1995,pp.223-228.

Montalvo, F.T and Torres M.C.G. 2004. Self regulated learning:current and future directions. Department of Education. Universidada de Navarra.Spain.

Hjelle, l.A., and Ziegler, D.J. 1981. Personality theories: basic assumptions, research, and applications. 2nd ed. Auckland: McGraw-Hill book Company.

Hosford, R.E. 1969. Behaviour Counselling: A contemporary overview, the counselling psychologist, 6, 1-33.

Lerner, J.W. 1988. Learning Disabilities: Theories, Diagnosis, and Teaching Strategies 5th Ed. Boston. Houghton Miffin Company.

Wong Bernice, YL. 1991. Learning About Learning Disabilities. 2nd Ed. United Kingdom. Academic Press, Inc.

Smith, S.L, Hoskins, J.L and Perez, E. Spring 2010, Issue 3. Vocabulary Instructional Strategies (Science Key Vocabulary Assessment~SKeVA~ Monitoring Science Success) de Bono, E. 1992. Teach your child how to think, London.: Viking Boorstin, D.J. 1985. The discoverers. New York: Vintage.

Index